Glimmers of Hope in a Darkening World

Donald DeMarco

Glimmers of Hope in a Darkening World

Designed by James Kent Ridley

Published by Goodboks Media

Printed in the U.S.A.

ISBN: 9798518129726

GOODBOOKS MEDIA

3453 Aransas

Corpus Christi, Texas, 78411

www.goodbookmedia.com

Dedication:

This book is dedicated to the memory of
Jacques Maritain,
truly a Pilgrim of the Absolute.

Epigraphs:

"The spiritual experience of the philosopher is the nourishing soil of philosophy; that without it there is no philosophy; and that, even so, spiritual experience does not, or must not, enter into the intelligible texture of philosophy. The pulp of the fruit must consist of nothing but the truth."

Jacques Maritain, *Existence & the Existent*

"Right now the whole world seems to be going through a dark night of the soul."

Flannery O'Connor

Acknowledgement:

I thank the editors of *Crisis, Catholic Exchange, The National Catholic Reporter,* and *The Wanderer* for granting permission to reprint some of the articles contained in this book. I also want to give special thanks to my eagle-eyed proof-reader, Jocelyn Pollard.

Kitchener, Ontario;
April 5, 2001 Easter Monday

Table of Contents

Hope:

DARKNESS

"Let there be Light" has two distinct meanings. The first refers to the sun and all of creation. If God presides over this Light, the Devil presides over Darkness as the Prince of Darkness. Light and darkness have nothing in common. Dark cannot banish darkness, only light can.

The second meaning refers to the light of the mind by which man can know the truth of things. Education, which is the illumination of the mind, is the passage from darkness to light. Truth, as Saint John Paul II states in his encyclical *Veritatis Splendor* has a certain "splendor" by which it can be known by the light of the mind. This light, however, is prone to being dimmed and even extinguished. Relativism and skepticism cause a dimming of the light. Deconstruction and nihilism bring about its extinction.

The world darkens when truth becomes less and less discernible. The truth will make us free, but the darkness that envelops us will produce confusion and chaos. In our darkening world the unborn child is no longer seen as human. The distinction between male and female blur into an amorphous cloud. God disappears and Scripture loses its meaning. We are left without guidance. In desperation, we use "choice" as a substitute for truth. Our windows to reality are replaced by sealed doors. We no longer know who we are.

We lack the light by which we can recognize that the darkness is dark and therefore a deprivation. We misname our predicament as "progress" or "liberation". We trade truth, justice, and beauty for diversity, equity, and inclusivity. We find ourselves back in Plato's cave, mesmerized by shadows, but fearful of the truth.

Philosophy is both the love of wisdom as well as the love of light. As the darkness increases, philosophy wanes. The philosophic enterprise, however, is our road back to a recovery of the light. The capacity to know the truth of things remains within us. It only needs to be rediscovered for the light by which we live, know, and love, to be rekindled.

Equality Without Windows

My daughter's high school required her to wear a navy blue cardigan sweater. So off we went to a clothing store so that she could be in full conformity with the school's dress code. The sales clerk, however, told us that none were in stock. Nonetheless, my daughter, while browsing, discovered exactly what she was looking for on the rack. "Oh, no", mustered the sales clerk, "that one is for boys, the one for girls has buttons and button holes on the reverse side". My daughter laughed. "Who's going to know the difference?"

Was this an instance of stressing the difference between boys and girls a bit too much? It was a time when women were discouraged from smoking cigarettes, but men found it cool to light up. Full court basketball was fine for boys, but considered too strenuous for girls who were not allowed to stray from one side of the court to the other, and were restricted to two dribbles per possession. Women wore makeup, men wore cologne. The male always led on the dance floor, women followed uncomplainingly. The suitor picked up the check; his date said, "Thank you, I had a wonderful evening". Men went off to war; women stayed home and prayed for their beloved heroes.

Those days may be gone forever. With the arrival of transgendered people, the difference between the sexes has been blurred to the point of no longer being recognized, let alone honored or ritualized. A bill has been introduced in California that would hit store owners with a $1,000 fine if they separated "toys for boys" from "toys for girls". In the interest of equality, the sexes are now regarded as identical. If one disagrees, there are penalties to be handed out. Nevertheless, the penalties for strict conformity will be far more severe.

The recent pro-abortion, LGBTQ *Equality Act* has been passed and pro-life leaders regard it as "the most comprehensive assault on Christianity ever written into law". Having abolished the distinction between male and female, biological males can use the locker rooms, restrooms and shower facilities that have always been reserved for females. The ramifications are extensive. According to Dr. Bill Donohue, Ph.D., pressure would be placed on Catholic foster care programs to conform or shut down: "They would either have to agree to allow two men to adopt children—a clear violation of Church teachings—or lose federal funding." Similar pressure would be placed on Catholic hospitals to perform abortions. Family Research Council (FRC) President Tony Perkins described the *Equality Act* as "a catastrophic loss of religious freedom in America."

In a senate hearing for the post of Assistant Secretary of Health, Senator Rand Paul (R-Kentucky) questioned Biden's nominee, who is a transgender woman. Rand offered an array of medical facts and personal testimonies underscoring the extreme inadvisability of performing genital mutilations of children who wanted to change their gender. The nominee, Dr.

Rachel Levine, persisted in refusing to answer the specific question, "Do you oppose the mutilation of the genitalia of children?" Rand also asked, "Do you support government overriding parental consent on puberty blockers?" In dodging the issue, Dr. Levine reiterated that such a procedure is "complex" and "nuanced".

The new notion of the equality between the sexes is exceedingly narrow. It is equality without windows. Men and women are certainly equal, but only in some ways. They are equal in humanity and equal under the law, to cite but two examples. But their equality has an altruistic side to it, which is akin to looking out the window and seeing a vast array of things. Equality is not incompatible with complementarity. In fact, and throughout history, complementarity has been a powerful and positive force in bringing men and women together and forming the basis of marriage and the family. The new notion of equality is stilted, truncated, reduced, emaciated, and without windows.

The notion of complementarity, so hateful to contemporary democrats, abortionists, and the LGBTQ consortium, gives added quality to mere equality. Men and women, according to no less an authority as *Genesis* were made with special differences so that they could fulfill each other. The man initiates, the woman receives. But his initiative need not be aggressive, nor is her receptivity necessarily passive. They are, as the poet Browning stated, "Two halves of a severed soul". Sociologist Margaret Mead contends that "If any human society . . . . . is to survive, it must have a pattern of social life that comes to terms with the differences between the sexes" (*Male and Female*, p. 173). Opposing these differences points toward cultural anarchy.

The notion of complementarity is a vital apart of the specific relationship that obtains between male and female. Parents and their children complement each other. The former bring their experience, love, and knowledge to their offspring who are in critical need of these gifts. Children, contrary to TV sitcoms, are not wiser and more capable than their parents. Teachers and students have a naturally complementary relationship. The art of teaching is different than the art of learning. The teacher is the motivator, the student is the ardent learner. The medical doctor is the complement of his patient. The patient does not make the diagnosis, or perform the surgery.

In general, the complementary relationship is mutually fulfilling. We all have needs that we cannot fulfill by ourselves. The concept of equality without windows is essentially anti-society as well as anti-personal. We live and grow and mature thanks to the benefits that we draw from our complementary opposites. And the most dynamic and universal of all of these relationships is complementarity of the sexes. Pope Saint John XXIII has expressed the matter simply and accurately: "Men and women are equal in dignity, complementary in mission."

Equality and the Loss of Identity

Philosophy is not the exclusive province of the specialist. It is for every thinking person. The problem lies in the fact that so many people do not know how to apply philosophy. Consider the notion of equality, for example. Many think that it is a free-floating value that does not require being rooted in something other than itself. As a result, they apply equality willy-nilly to areas where things are not equal. The unfortunate consequence of this reckless application of equality is, in many cases, the loss of identity. In this sense, therefore, applying equality where it does not belong can be destructive.

Equality is justified when it is anchored in truth. At mealtime, servings of food should be proportioned to each individual at the table. The child and the adults will not have equal amounts of food because their needs are not the same. The truth of each individual is the measure of how much they are able to eat. Likewise, clothing is tailored to fit the size and shape of the body. Just as not everyone will eat equal amounts of food, not everyone will wear the same size clothes. Detached from truth, equality is fit for mayhem. Consequently, it is now politically correct to hold that same-sex "marriages" and traditional marriages are equal. In the *Revolt of the Masses* Jose Ortega y Gasset spoke knowingly about the "sovereignty of the masses".

Being in love with equality while rejecting truth is like wanting a car but not wanting to pay for it or hoping to become a doctor but avoiding medical school. Truth is the justifying source for equality. Equality is not self-justifying. This, one might think, is a simple enough principle, but it has remained elusive through the ages. Voltaire, in the 18th century, saw fit to distinguish equality from various forms of inequality that are mistaken for equality by offering a statement that should be regarded as a model of irresistible common sense:

> They who say all men are equal speak an undoubted truth; if they mean that all men have an equal right to liberty, to their property and to their protection of the laws. But they are mistaken if they think that men are equal in their station and employments, since they are not so by their talents.

The distinguished legal scholar, Robert H. Bork observed how such personally identifying characteristic as status, talent, and achievement were being sacrificed on the altar of radical equality:

> The sixties rebels attacked hierarchies and lines of authority resulting from merit and achievement. They wanted parity with the faculty, an end to grading, admissions on the basis of race, and the right to participate in the governance and alteration of academic institutions they did not understand and would be in for only a few years.

The immediate consequence of such radical egalitarianism is the loss of identity marked by personal achievement, status, and special talents. The distinctions would be obliterated between teacher and student, artist and pedestrian, the ruler and the ruled. Parity might be a good ideal for the National Football League, but when it is applied to all human beings it abolishes what makes them distinct and reduces them to the lowest common denominator.

The zeal for equalizing virtually everything became entrenched in the minds of university students to the point that they regarded it as a self-evident first principle. Philosopher Allan Bloom, author of the best-selling *The Closing of the American Mind*, pointed out that

> [I]t is almost inconceivable to them [university students] that there can be a theoretical questioning of the principle

of equality, let alone a practical doubt about it.

From a common sense point of view, we should rejoice in the fact that other people do any number of things better than we can do them ourselves. Personally, I am both indebted to and grateful for athletes, musicians, carpenters, plumbers, electricians, engineers, writers, doctors and nurses who are better than I am in their respective fields. We are equal as human beings but unequal in talent and achievement. To allow radical equality to blot out personal accomplishment represents a terrible loss for all of us.

Nonetheless, the siren song of egalitarianism continues to mes-

merize people who think they are being progressive. As the new year of 2021 rings in, House Speaker Nancy Pelosi is praising a new proposal that would "honor all gender identities by changing pronouns and familiar relationships in the House rules to be gender neutral". Thus, gendered terms such as father, mother, son, daughter, brother, sister, uncle, aunt, nephew, niece, husband, wife, etc. would be removed. In their place would be such terms as parent, child, sibling, spouse, parent's sibling, and so on. A husband loses his identity as a husband and become his spouse's spouse. An uncle ceases to be an uncle as he becomes related to his sibling's child. Likewise, an aunt also metamorphoses into a person related to her sibling's child.

Nieces and nephews disappear. A mother-in-law dissolves into a parent-in-law.

Pelosi regards this language change as "bold". Others my view it merely as a cowardly capitulation to political correctness. She also hails it as "visionary". Yet, how "visionary" is it to become blind to the distinctions between husband and wife, brother and sister, uncle and aunt, nephew and niece? In addition, she lauds it as "transparent". What seems to be transparent is transparent nonsense. The new language would bring about a loss of specific identities such as mother, father, brother sister, husband, and wife.

God and the Catholic Church asks us to be saints. The saint will not compare himself to others who may not have reached a level of sanctity, but he will acknowledge that thanks to God's grace, he is a better person than he once was. Here is an inequality that paves the road to salvation. Being bold and progressive means being more holy. To remain equal with one's self is to be sterile. Life demands that we become a better person today than what we were yesterday.

Should Scripture Be More Trans-Friendly?

The Brighton and Sussex University Hospitals (UK) have issued a new set of guidelines that introduces an assortment of trans-friendly terms. The concern is to avoid offending people who have been trans-gendered by insisting that there is such a thing as distinct sexes. The guidelines instruct doctors, nurses, and midwives to use gender neutral terms. Thus, "chestfeeding" should replace breastfeeding so that nursing a baby is not necessary associated with a particular sex. Breast milk gives way to "chest milk" or "human milk". The person engaged in giving "chest milk should be known as a "birthing parent," rather than as a mother. Pregnant women should be called "pregnant persons" and the father as the "second biological parent".

As everyone who has the slightest knowledge of human anatomy knows, breast milk does not come directly from the chest. But in what is now called the "Post-Truth Era," truth must take a back seat to gender ideology. Both men and women have chests. In this sense, they are both equal. To make the breastfeeding mother distinctive could be offensive to trans-gendered people who do not want to be excluded. Nonetheless, despite the commitment to be inclusive, reality indicates that the man is excluded from breastfeeding while the mother's act of breastfeeding is denied. This should be offensive to mothers who are nursing their babies.

Rodney Dangerfield, whose character never got any respect, traced his malady to the fact that he was breastfed by his father. What was once understood clearly a joke is now regarded as a welcomed example of inclusivity. What is comedy's loss is gender neutral's gain.

Meanwhile, the Australia National University's *Gender Institute Handbook* suggests that "gestational parent" is preferable to "mother," while "non-birthing parent" should replace "father". How far this trend will go is difficult to say. Perhaps "Mother's Day" will give way to "Gestational Parent's Day". In that case, a child might be able to purchase a mug dedicated to "The World's Best Gestater". Appropriate mugs could be designed for "The World's Best Second Biological Parent". The terms "Mom" and "Dad" would be expunged from the vernacular. Children would attend sensitivity training classes.

No doubt there will be people who would like to see Holy Scripture changed to accommodate the transgendered brigade. Genesis would state that God created "people" who could get together in different ways. Male, female, husband, wife, and marriage would be deleted. The Nursing Madonna would be known as the "Chestfeeding Person". St. Paul would address his readers with the salutation, "Dear Siblings". There would be no marriage at Cana, just a gathering of people for no particular reason.

Traditionally, reality came first and words were intended to mirror reality. Anatomists would recognize the nursing function of the mammary glands and refer to it as "breastfeeding". In the brave new world, an arbitrary ideology comes first, which does not reflect reality, and words are used to mirror that ideology. This, of course, is a formula for chaos, since not everyone will begin with the same ideology. Reality would no longer be a common denominator. Nonetheless, "Big Brother" will be watching.

In the world of gender neutrality, there is no way to specify one's niece, nephew, aunt or uncle. If one refers to "my secondary biological parent's sibling's child", the identity of niece or nephew remains obscure. Similarly, is my "primary birthing parent's sibling" my aunt or my uncle? And is her "sibling" her brother or her sister.

The vocabulary of politically correct terms, such as "trans-friendliness," "gender neutrality," "diversity", "inclusivity," and "equity," fail to place dialogue at the starting point. To speak of breastfeeding as chestfeeding is to move a significant step away from reality. The science of anatomy would need to be made less clear. A process of education in reverse gear would ensue. Would a return to reality be possible? Ideology comes at a high price.

Religion, commands us that we not offend God. If we carry

out that mandate, we have no need to worry about offending anyone, since all human beings are children of God. Christ commands us to love our neighbor. This is a positive command and a good starting point. Not offending anyone, is a negative mandate which neglects the positive mandate that should precede it. Even if we could avoid offending anyone, we might still be in the dark about what we should do. We need to act, and not offending is not an act. A life that avoids offending people but never cares about them is sterile and empty. One cannot cultivate flowers by plucking out weeds.

Holy Scripture makes no concessions to political correctness. It puts first things first. It honors the primacy of God, truth, and love. In yielding to political correctness we avoid what comes first and are lost without a compass. Scripture is our compass because it invariably points us in the right direction.

Why the Negative Is a Positive

Pope Francis declared on Monday, March 22, 2001 that the Catholic Church will not bless same-sex unions since God "cannot bless sin." The two-page document also noted that the Church welcomes the blessing of people who are homosexual, but not same-sex unions that involve sexual acts that the Church has never condoned either for homosexual or heterosexual people. The declaration is nothing new.

Nonetheless, the Pontiff's statement, and predictably, has created an international storm of protest. A significant number of bishops in Germany have dissented from it and have pledged to bless same-sex unions on a continuing basis. Many Catholics have interpreted the statement as God turning His back on people who are involved in a same-sex "marriage". Anger, resentment, disappointment, and bitterness reign.

Priests from the Missionary Society of St. Paul the Apostle in parishes in New York, Boston, and Los Angeles have openly criticized the Pope's statement. While saints such as Augustine held that once "Rome has spoken, the case is closed," one Paulist Father said, instead of closing the matter, the Congregation of the Doctrine of the Faith Declaration has "opened up a volcano."

One important factor that is at stake in the imbroglio is the integrity of the sacraments. This is a matter of great significance. In the traditional form of confession (reconciliation) the penitent says, "Bless me father for I have sinned". This acknowledgment of having sinned is combined with a firm purpose of amendment. Only then can the sacrament be administered. The sacrament of reconciliation prepares the way for the proper reception of the Eucharist.

Same-sex marriages involve sexual acts which are forbidden even to heterosexual married couples. The intention to perform illicit sexual acts closes the door to a blessing. It is as if a same-sex partner said, "Bless me father for I intend to sin, and have absolutely no desire to amend my life." Under such circumstances, a blessing could not be given. In the parable of the sower, the seeds that fall on thorns or rocks do not germinate (Matthew 13:1-23; Mark 4: 1-20; Luke 8:1-15). The intention to sin and the refusal to amend one's life makes a mockery of the sacrament of reconciliation. Thus, the Pope's declaration is most positive in that it protects the value of the sacraments. It is also positive in the sense that it encourages people to abandon sin and lead a more moral life.

Many same-sex couples will inevitably deny that their sexual acts are sinful, but are really "loving". Nonetheless, we know that certain acts, such as sodomy, transmit diseases. AIDS has claimed the lives of millions of people throughout the world. It is not a loving act to dispose a person to disease and possibly death. The Church must not discriminate. She cannot approve certain sexual acts for some people while prohibiting them from others. It is the same with all other sins. Thievery, for example, is a sin no matter whether the thief is hetero- or homosexual.

Homosexual individuals are themselves deeply divided on these issues although only one-side gets press coverage. The Church cannot bend its moral teachings, which are based on the natural law, to political demands. John McKellor, a self-admitted homosexual, founded HOPE (Homosexuals Opposed to Political Extremism) in order to combat "the lies, myths, distortions, and propaganda of modern gay activism." He warns that a disregard for the natural law, to which we are all bound, invites social calamity.

Bishop Joseph Strickland of Texas, has hailed the Pope's declaration as a "bold stand for truth". It is "bold" since Pope Francis could expect a strong backlash. But the truth is far more important than capitulation to error. The notion of not offering a blessing seems, at first blush, harsh and insensitive until we realize that same-sex couples do not want a blessing since the proper disposition for receiving a blessing is a firm commitment not to continue sinning. His Excellency believes the faithful need clarification from the hierarchy "because we're in a time of a lot of confusion, even within the Church at times." The truth, as Christ said, is like a sword: "Do not think I came to bring peace on earth; I came to bring not peace, but a sword" (Matthew 10:34).

We are confronted with a clash between truth and sentimentality. In a world ruled by sentimentality, everything is "nice". It is a utopia in which there is no sin and everyone accepts everyone. C. S. Lewis had a more trenchant notion of what it is like to be "nice" and only "nice". In his novel, *That Hideous Strength* (1945), he presents N.I.C.E. as "The National Institute for Coordinated Experiments" which is a front for sinister supernatural forces. If the truth is not nice, it is because it is liberating. And there are many people who simply do not want to be liberated. Liberation simply requires too much honesty and too much effort.

We are revisiting the Pelagian heresy of the fifth century that affirmed the essential goodness of human nature and denied the Church's doctrine of Original Sin. Celestius, a disciple of Pelagius, denied the necessity if infant baptism. One wonders what else must transpire in a world, which Gibbons characterized as a "chronicle of crimes and follies," to convince people that evil exists and we need help from above?

Protecting the integrity of the sacraments is surely something positive. Wanting to help people must be complemented by knowing how to help them. Giving in to their demands is not necessarily helping them. The road to reform is not easy. It is like recovery after surgery. What is truly negative is the backlash against the Church and Catholics who want to help others. They are allegedly homophobic, ignorant, and fearful. To set the record straight – the Church is positive; its detractors are negative.

Letter from an Atheist

I had an article published in our local newspaper in which I made the point in passing that the ultimate source of all authority is God. What I assumed to be a benign, and certainly not an inflammatory remark, nonetheless inflamed a local atheist who saw fit to dispatch an angry letter to me. Before opening the envelope that bore an address I did not recognize, I noticed the words: "Nothing Fails Like Prayer!" My thoughts immediately turned to a recent conference on cancer held in Kingston, Ontario. One of the participating scientists stated that the only factor we can be sure about that benefits cancer patients in the recovery of their health is prayer. Her claim was supported by statistical data. I thought it rather curious that someone would use envelopes to beseech the world not to pray.

In reading the letter I discovered that I was accused of "making irrelevant and spurious character assaults" against all atheists. I was also guilty of making "nonsensical" and "unsubstantiated claims". My atheist advisor informed me

WITHOUT GOD,
I HAVE NO REASON
TO BE MORAL.

that if I contend that God is the ultimate source of moral authority, then I implied that those who do not believe in God have no basis for their authority and consequently are immoral.

Was I accusing atheists of being immoral? An atheist may be loving, decent, and honorable without recognizing that these virtues ultimately come from God. A desert dweller who has never seen rain may believe that the ultimate source of water is the local oasis. I was really making no accusations, just stating my view that God is the ultimate source of morality. Not being able to see something is no reason to deny its existence. We neither see not can conceptualize the electron. Yet, it is so well known through its effects that we utilize it to illuminate our cities, guide our planes through night skies, and make the most accurate measurements. As astrophysicist Wernher von Braun has remarked,

> What strange rationale makes some physicists accept the inconceivable electron as real, while refusing to accept the reality of God on the ground that they cannot conceive Him?

An atheist may have invisible means of support even if he is unaware of them.

I have always found it odd that a person who neither believes in God, the supernatural, the immortality of the soul, the consolation of religion, and so on, could be apostolic about such emptiness. It is as if a person discovered a formula for despair and was most eager to share it with everyone, even at his own expense. The atheist is content with the idea that we evolved from mud and slime and shuns the notion that a human being is made in the image of God.

My atheist apologist is a member of the Freedom From Religion Foundation. In keeping with his apostolic zeal, he included information about how and at what price I could become a supporter of "freethought" and a subscriber to *Freethought Today*, allegedly "the only freethought newspaper in the United States". Apparently my thoughts are not free if they lead me to a conviction that God exists, which I freely maintain. Are the freethought people promoting freedom of thought or are they simply advancing atheism? When thought is truly free, it could go in any direction. Should not thought be circumscribed by truth?

I opened one of the pamphlets that came with the letter: *Nontract No. 3* as it is called. I was greeted by the phrase, "We are all born atheists". The authors may have been familiar with the opening line of Jean-Jacques Rousseau's *Social Contract:* "Man is born free". The plain truth is that we come into the world neither atheists nor free. A newborn is neither an atheist nor a theist. He has not given such matters any thought. Should atheism, therefore, be equated with ignorance as well as not thinking at all? What happened to the requirement of being a free thinker?

I read further and was told that among the great artists who exemplified the spirit of the skeptic or the freethinker and refused to bend to religion is Alfred Lord Tennyson. This was not a good choice, I thought. The most often quoted line from the pen of the great Victorian poet is a glowing testimony to prayer: "More things are wrought by prayer than this world dreams of". Scholars have hailed Tennyson's great poem *In Memoriam* as the most dramatic as well as the most religious of English elegies. Queen Victoria, upon losing her husband, stated that *In Memoriam* was her comfort, second only to the Bible.

Consider the following quatrain from its Prologue:

> We have but faith: we cannot know;
> For knowledge is of things we see;
> And yet we trust it comes from thee,
> A beam in darkness: let it grow.

The rest of my atheist's material was equally uneven and unconvincing.

Theism and atheism do not exclude each other completely. The believer and the unbeliever share both belief and doubt. Even saints were tempted to disbelieve. The believer is not entirely free of doubt; the unbeliever is not entirely free of belief. I began to think that my apologist for atheism was trying to defend himself against belief that kept tormenting him, like the *Hound of Heaven*. Perhaps, if he could purge others from their beliefs he would find his own belief more easy to accept. Having read his arguments, it seemed only too clear that he had erected a house of cards which he hoped that I would evaluate as a fortress of steel.

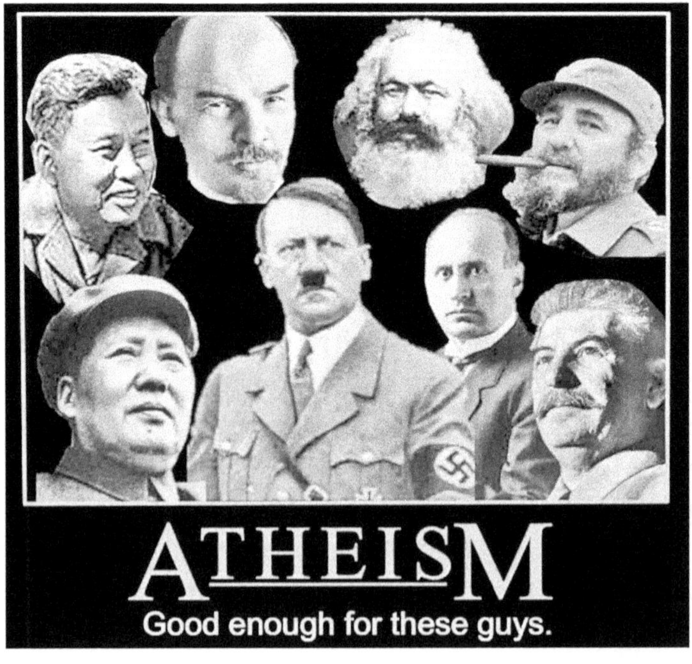

UNREASON

We are rational human beings by nature, but often behave as anything but rational in practice. This is a great misfortune inasmuch as reason is the very faculty which allows all people of the world to communicate meaningfully to each other. Without the exercise of reason, we live in a Tower of Babel.

Reason and will should be harmoniously related to each other. However, the will often finds what reason discerns as disagreeable and takes flight from reason. We deny what we do not like and retreat to a world of illusions. But when we try to live by will alone, we find that we have lost our common basis with others. The result of this alienation is misunderstanding, confusion, and violence. We have ears but cannot hear, eyes but cannot see. Inevitably unreason replaces reason and, in our common blindness, fall into a pit.

Reason is our only passage to reality. If we are sick, we must recognize that fact and proceed to seek a remedy. There is no advantage in denying that fact and creating an illusion for ourselves. An unwanted pregnancy can cause great turmoil, but denying the nature of the unborn child or the problems that abortion can cause, leads away from reality and into a world where no help is available.

Unreason results when the will supplants reason. The proper function of the will, however, is to serve reason, not to gain dominion over the person. Irrational behavior is not helpful to anyone. It is, to us a term that has not lost its significance, "mindless". The state of mindlessness remains free of politically correct distortions. No one wants to be called mindless, though many continue to act mindlessly.

Reality presents us with many disagreeable facts. In the face of reality we need an arsenal of virtues, which, collectively, supply us with "character". It is purely sentimental to think that we can live a life without ever being offended, or ever being prevented from achieving what we want. If we want to remain real, we must remain reasonable.

Hardening of the Mind

A friend and I were discussing the abortion issue with a young lady. We had emphasized the importance of reason. She was intrigued by what we were saying, which seemed entirely new to her. Looking at us with a sense of expectation, she asked, "What is reason?"

We are, supposedly, rational creatures. Reason should not be alien to us. However, our culture often stresses feeling to the point of excluding reason or at least dimming our awareness of what reason is. I do not think that our response to her question was very satisfactory. Reason, to put it in simplest terms, is the passage to reality. Without utilizing reason, we remain stranded within ourselves, dislocated from the shores of reality. How does such an anomaly come about?

The Greeks, who advanced philosophy, were also aware of a condition called "*scotosis*". This word is defined as "intellectual blindness" or "the hardening of the mind against unwanted wisdom". Psychologists sometimes refer to it as "cognitive dissonance". It is instructive to know that even members of SCOTUS can be stricken with *scotosis*.

Sancta Syncletica

Amma Syncletica was a Christian saint and Desert Mother from Roman Egypt in the 4th century. She sheds some important light on the subject. "It is impossible for us," she states, "to be surrounded by worldly honor and at the same time to bear heavenly fruit." We cannot expect to be mired in the City of Man and represent the wisdom of the City of God. Saint John Paul II warned his beloved priests that "In the absence of deep inner life, a priest will imperceptibly turn into an office clerk".

Reality is what existed before we arrived. Therefore, in no sense does it depend on us. In a sense, reality is "opposed" to us. If we are to know anything in its truth, it is that which is outside of us that we know. Bernard of Clairvaux put it clearly when he said that

> In our doing and acting everything depends on this, that we comprehend objects clearly and treat them according to their nature.

If we are to be realistic, we must see things in their objectivity.

When Christ says, "He who has ears to hear, let him hear," he is distinguishing between perception and understanding (Mark 4:9; Matthew 11:15,). The mere use of the ear is perception. But perception is not the same as understanding what

Christ is teaching. Those who accept the word "will bear fruit, thirtyfold and sixtyfold and a hundredfold" (Mark 4: 20). But with regard to others, "the cares of the world, and the delight in riches, and the desire for other things, enter in and choke the word, and it proves unfruitful" (Mark 4:19). We may also add, "those who have eyes, let them see" without compromising Christ's message.

There will always be some who perceive the word but do not understand or accept it, just as there will always be some who see things in their objectivity, which is to say, in their truth. The abortion issue provides an example where *scotosis* is a common malady. Yet there are many who see abortion for what it is. Helen Alvaré, Professor of Law at George Mason University, dares to reveal its truth. "The government is essentially proclaiming," she writes, "that there is only one legitimate kind of homicide in the U. S.: killing within the family" (*The National Catholic Register* Jan. 31-Feb. 13).

What she is saying is that abortion is a form of domestic violence. And she is right. It is certainly "domestic" since it involves the mother and her child; it is certainly violent since it results in the death of the unborn child. How many of those who promote abortion can see this horrifying truth? The only way they can maintain their position is to be blind to its reality. They withdraw from objectivity and rename abortion in an entirely subjective sense as a "choice," a "remedy," or even as a "right". At the same time, they are obliged to castigate defenders of life in any number of demeaning terms.

Scripture tells us that the pharaoh suffered from a hardening of the heart. The root of this hardening may very well be a hardening of the mind.

> The eye is the lamp of the body. So, if your eye is sound, your whole body will be full of light; but if your eye is not sound, your whole body will be full of darkness. If then the

> light in you is darkness, how great is the darkness? (Matthew 6:22-24).

It is an American tragedy that, concerning abortion, *scotosis* is afflicting lawyers and politicians in high places. We must remain faithful to the truth, however, and trust that the light of truth will finally be recognized so that it can lead to a freedom in which no one will need to be executed.

The Truth Will Make You Flee

"The truth will make you odd," wrote Flannery O'Connor. For Ralph Waldo Emerson, God has given us a choice between truth and repose. We cannot have both. "Truth is incontrovertible," stated Winston Churchill, "Panic may resent it, ignorance may deride it, malice may distort it, but there it is." Truth is the first casualty of war. In contrast with these remarks, Christ reminds us that "the truth shall set you free" (John 8:32).

With regard to solving the race problem, it appears that the truth, which is resented, derided, and distorted, makes people flee. Renowned surgeon, Dr. Ben Carson has pointed out an unpalatable truth, namely, that the Media is relentlessly promoting white guilt along with black victimization. Today's whites are made to feel guilty about how their ancestors of hundreds of years ago treated black slaves. At the same time, blacks are made to feel that their victimization is ongoing. This is far from the truth of things and only delays the real work that must be done in order to expunge racism from American culture.

Thomas Sowell, is a Senior Fellow at Stanford University's Hoover Institute. He is the author of a plethora of books on economics and social theory. He points out that as late as the 1950's "only 18% of black households were single parent". Today, he avers, the majority of black children (66%) are raised by a single parent. And among black families in poverty, 85% of children have no father. This backslide, according to Sowell is the result of a government welfare state that creates a mentality of dependence. This dependence is inimical to personal motivation. Why work when you can have something for nothing? Racism is not the cause.

It appears that in many instances, racism is detected where it does not exist and suppressed where it does exist. Speculating without truth can lead to strange conclusions. The notion that racism against blacks is "systemic" is a fabrication that further feeds white guilt and black victimhood. The notion that there could be prejudice against whites is politically incorrect to the point of being virtually unthinkable.

The CEO of Catholic Charities of Eastern Washington has made an astonishing confession to the world. "I am a racist," he states, "My Catholic Church, and my Catholic Charities organization, is racist. How could they not be? Our Catholic faith tradition is built on the premise that a baby, born in a manger in the Middle East, was a white baby." In so saying, he is identifying racism with skin color. Therefore, everyone with skin color is a racist. Yet people cannot change their color any more than a tiger can change its stripes. Racism is not genetic. It is an attitude. Does this even need to be stated? If all whites are racists, does that mean that all blacks are racists as well?

Jodi Shaw, an employee of Smith College in Northampton, Massachusetts, has resigned her post, accusing the elite women's college of creating a "racially hostile environment against white people". She testified that because she was "white," her discomfort "was framed as an act of aggression". The college has adopted "critical race theory," a quasi-Marxist ideology which has been spreading across American institutions. It sets "oppressors" and "oppressed" against each other on the basis of skin color – whites vs. other races. "Under the guise of racial progress," Shaw stated, "Smith College has created a racially hostile environment in which individual acts of discrimination and hostility flourish".

An article in *Epoch Times* (Feb. 25—March 3, 2021) carries an exposé about how Coca-Cola employees are required to take a training course on how to be "less white". An on-line training program is titled, *Confronting Racism. Understanding what it means to be white. Challenging what it means to be racist.* Whites are encouraged to be less arrogant, more humble, and to "break with white solidarity". Attorney Harmeet K. Dhillon has stated that the slides appear to show "blatant racial discrimination" against white people. Political commentator Candace Owens urged employees to file lawsuits against the corporation. It is easy to imagine that society would implode if blacks were systematically urged to be "less black". Like Smith College, Coca-Cola is taking its a page from "critical race theory".

Zeal without restraint can be counterproductive. The Oregon Department of Education has encouraged its teachers to enroll in a course entitled, *A Pathway to Equitable Math Instruction.* The 82-page guide warns teachers that identifying mathematical mistakes with "wrongness" and focusing on the right answers are practices that "perpetuate white supremacy culture". In order to promote "Equitable Math," however, the Department of Education would need to suppress history. "Algebra" is a word of Arabic etymology. Arabic mathematicians are famous for their work in algebra, number theory, and number systems. They also made important contributions to geometry, trigonometry, and mathematical astronomy. It would be ludicrous to blame them for promoting white supremacy. In addition, courses in physics and engineering would need to be suppressed since the correct answers in those fields are absolutely necessary for safe technology.

No one is opposed to improving race relations. The start of this revolution that stands to benefit everyone, however, is not some hare-brain ideology or an obsession with finding racism everywhere, but with truth. And yet, truth is avoided. In fact, people are fleeing from the truth. There are many individuals of different skin color who are making a sincere attempt to call attention to the truth, but their voices are being drowned by the Major Media that prefers sensationalism and whatever happens to be the reigning ideology.

Christ's words remain as both intellectually sound as well as practically efficient: "The truth shall set you free".

The Futility of Slogans

Ted Koppel, who gained fame as the anchor for ABC's *Nightline*, delivered a commencement address to the graduating class of Duke University in Durham, North Carolina. His presentation was not the usual politically correct palaver. Among his many trenchant remarks was the assertion that "We have actually convinced ourselves that slogans will save us". Koppel's address was in 1987. We have not yet weaned ourselves of this delusion. We continue to believe that slogans will save us.

Mr. Koppel may have either disturbed or enlightened his audience by pointing out that moral truths are hard to come by and often looked upon with suspicion. "In its purest form," he said, "truth is not a polite tap on the shoulder. It is a howling reproach. What Moses brought down from Mount Sinai were not the Ten Suggestions".

National basketball players, in a feeble effort to achieve racial equality, were sporting the message, Black Lives Matter on their warmup shirts. Basketball courts were festooned with the same slogan. This proved to be somewhat controversial,

even among blacks. It also seemed excessively narrow. After all, non-Blacks make up the bulk of the world's population. Consequently, they changed their slogan to "Now is the time to make justice for everyone". This, unfortunately, although more universal, is an awkward phrase. Justice has nothing to do with the calendar. Justice is never out of season. Moreover, justice is not something we "make" but exercise on a person-to person basis. It is a personal virtue that is not easily attained. Nor, if attained, is it easily retained. Law students spend years of training to become ambassadors of justice. And yet, there are lawyers who stray outside of the law. We need something a little more rigorous than slogans to form character.

Another problem with slogans is that they can serve nefarious purposes. Nike's slogan is "just do it," a suggestion that has no boundaries. Cigarette slogans, before they were removed by law, were instrumental in the development of lung cancer. Ashley Madison is a Toronto organization that promotes and arranges adultery. Its slogan is "life is short, have an affair". St. Thomas Aquinas pointed out that adultery is an act of injustice toward one's spouse. According to the *Catholic Catechism* (2335):

> Adultery is an injustice. He who commits adultery fails in his commitment. He does injury to the sign of the covenant which the marriage bond is, transgresses the rights of the other spouse, and undermines the institution of marriage by breaking the contract on which it is based. He

> compromises the good of human generation and the welfare of children who need their parents' stable union.

We may question whether those who work for racial justice are also working for marital fidelity? Justice has both breadth and depth.

While slogans may appeal to those who prefer not to think, they do little to feed the mind. Professor Martha Nussbaum, Distinguished Service Professor of Law and Ethics at the University of Chicago, has made the comment that:

> Every single university student should study philosophy. You need to lead the examined life and question your beliefs. If you don't learn critical thinking, then political debate degenerates into a contest of slogans.

We should be more suspicious of slogans than we are of philosophy. Socrates, Plato and Aristotle were not sloganeers. To profit from their wisdom, however, requires, time, effort, and reflection. The slogan, however, fits neatly into our fast paced society. Slogans distract us so that we do not see the truth. But it is the truth that shall make us free.

In his *Commentary on Job* (34, lect. 2) Aquinas states that one reason that men fall short of justice is "deference to the mob". Political correctness is a kind a mob psychology. We can easily be intimidated by trends, fashions, and everything that is *au courant*. We are social beings and do want to be "with it". The temptation to go along with others can be very seductive.

Justice, desirable as it is, is not an entrance value. We cannot begin our moral life with justice. Although we are bound to our neighbor by invisible cords of justice, it is not likely that we will be just to our neighbor if we do not have at least some regard for him. Therefore, justice presupposes love. In the absence of love, justice is merely a cold requirement, sometimes often imposed by the magistrate. We cannot love everyone passionately, but, according to the Christian mandate, we can love others justly. If I owe a stranger $100, I am indebted to pay him that sum. It is not likely that we will be just to people if we have absolutely no regard for them.

Here we get to the nub of the social problem. We need love before we can enact justice or, as a matter of fact, any other virtue. Moreover, slogans will not help in this regard. The family, as Saint John Paul II has often said, is the first school of love. In this sense, the family is indispensable. Parental love never has had a need to utilize slogans. Love develops through loving experiences.

It would be a mistake to think that justice is primarily a reaction to injustice. Often, this reaction takes the form of vengeance. True justice is both supported and nourished by love. What is egregiously missing in our current society is enough love that will inspire a plethora of other virtues, including courage, temperance, prudence, generosity, gratitude, compassion, and hope. The responsibility for restoring society does not lie with the NBA, but with the family.

Loose Thinking and Lost Logic

Loose thinking occurs when more is attributed to a subject than what the subject contains. For example, the U.S. Constitution does not include any provision for justifying abortion or same-sex marriage. You cannot extract a litre of water from a bottle that contains only a pint. Barack Obama offered us an excellent example of loose thinking when he defended the legalization of same-sex marriage by stating that it is about time that someone can marry the person he loves. Marriage contains marital love, but not all forms of love. Love is far more inclusive than marriage. We can love our parents, siblings, children, and married friends, but we cannot marry them. Marriage demands love, but love does not demand marriage. If one's belt is too loose, his pants will not stay up; if his reasoning is too loose, his arguments will not hold up. Loose talk starts rumors that are devoid of truth. A sound argument respects truth and is prepared to exclude what is irrelevant.

There is an art to loose thinking. If one cannot come up with a good argument to defend a position, he may use sheer rhetoric to take its place. Obama's notion of marriage succeeded in convincing many of his supporters. When Edmund Burke stated that the "study of law sharpens the mind by narrowing it," he was referring to the fact that the law involves only the things that are relevant. The law convicts the guilty, not the suspects.

Currently an altercation rages among members of the Toronto Catholic District School Board. The controversial issue centers on whether sexual orientation, gender identity, and family status (LGBTQ) should be added to the list of protected classes. Michael Del Grande, a lone dissenter, maintained that

the board has a responsibility to uphold Catholic moral teaching. He argued that if we continue to add things that are at odds with the Catholic Catechism, where do we stop? We will open ourselves to any number of immoralities, he stated, perhaps even "bestiality and vampirism". His reduction *ad absurdum* backfired. His opponents did not see the logic behind his argument. In addition, LGBTQ activists targeted Del Grande, making the complaint that his remarks, logical though they were, violated the Code of Conduct. In agreement with LGBTQ, but neither logic nor the Catholic Catechism, board members voted 8-I (Del Grande was not allowed to vote) to censure and impose sanctions on him. Campaign Life Coalition commented on the fiasco saying that "this board is in open rebellion against the moral teaching of the Catholic Church".

The Toronto Catholic School Board illustrates a widespread problem that exists among "liberal" Catholics, one that may be characterized as featuring a combination of loose thinking with lost logic. The *Catholic Catechism* is relevant to everyone. Therefore, it is truly catholic. It does not, however, single out individuals who have a particular lifestyle. Nor does it single out people who belong to a certain profession, such as medicine, law, education, and so on. If it accepted every lifestyle, it would have nothing to say. But it does have something to say, especially when it distinguishes between moral and immoral activities.

Loose thinking with regard to the *Catholic Catechism* aims at being broad-minded and inclusive to the point that contradicts what it should defend. Many Catholics who uphold Catholic teaching, such as Michael Del Grande, are presently regarded as pariahs, roadblocks in the path of progress. At the same time, Del Grande is contemplating launching defamation suits against those who have slandered him. Catholic trustees ought to be able to get along with each other without the need for legal action. One does not need to read the *Catechism* to understand that.

In his logically sensible book, *The Day Is Now Far Spent*, Robert Cardinal Sarah strongly rejects the notion that we can profit by affirming something that is not there:

> If I say that two plus two makes five or four and a half, am I freer? Rather, I am more idiotic. Freedom is essentially connected to the truth.

I am not more free nor more liberal nor more broad-minded if I affirm something that is not grounded in truth. In fact, I would be living in a dream world.

Logic is for everyone, atheists as well as theists. Bertrand Russell was a resolute atheist, but a superb logician. If logic is contradicted, it is highly unlikely that something more complicated, such as the Catholic Catechism will make any sense. In fact, when logic is violated, nothing makes any sense. Logic courses should be available at every Catholic institution of higher learning. A Catholic should be logical, in addition to being faithful. But it is quite another thing to develop sufficient moral integrity to perform one's duty as a member of a Catholic school board.

The Perilous Slide from Sentiment to Sentimentality

A sentiment is an emotion or a feeling that can be the basis of an idea. Sentimentality is an emotion or feeling that is closed in on itself. The sentimentalist is locked up in his own feelings, severed from a world which may be perceived as too harsh. Synonyms for sentimental include "gushy," "sugary," "cloying," "maudlin," and "mawkish". Sentimentality is fine as far as it goes, but it should not go very far. One cannot build an adequate philosophy of love on pure sentimentality. Love soon encounters practical imperatives. And yet, this attitude of sentimentality can be highly seductive.

Consider the 73rd Quatrain of Omar Khayyam's immortal *Rubaiyat*:

Ah Love! Could thou and I with Fate conspire
To grasp this sorry Scheme of Things entire,
Would not we shatter it to bits – and then
Re-mould it nearer to the Heart's Desire!

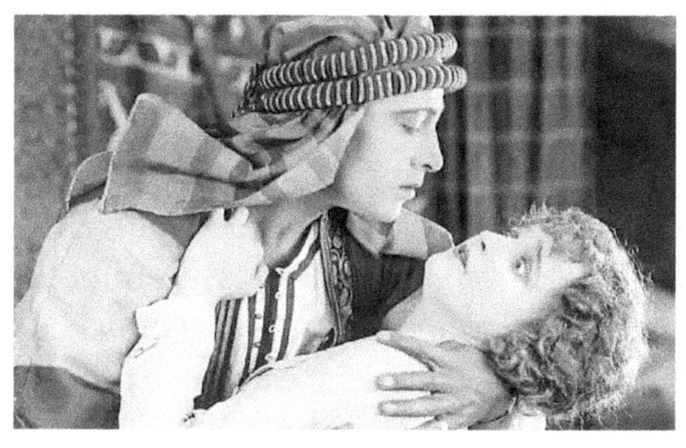

The world is a nightmare of madness and misery. Would it not be wonderful if we could create a new order which is congruent with the ecstasy of love that we experience this moment? If only this moment could last forever! We are not happy with the world that was given to us. Let us remake it in accordance with our wishes.

This quatrain is elegantly expressed and is worthy of its acclaim as a truly beautiful example of poetry. One has no quarrel with the sentiment it evokes. But if taken too seriously, it degenerates into sentimentality. The reason for this is twofold. First, recreating the world according to one's wishes is not possible. Sentimentality, being essentially a dreamy wishfulness, cannot cross the bridge that takes us into a new reality. Feeling apart from reason is incapable of building a better world. The second problem is that it represents either a rejection or a denial of God. Beautiful as the poem is, it is set in the context of Fate. God either does not exist or He is a very inadequate Creator. If He does exist, why did He not create a world closer to our hearts' desire? If He does not exist, then there is no hope for any of us.

Atheism lies at the bottom of the slide from sentiment to sentimentality. People reject God because they reject a world that contains too much suffering and does not mirror their feelings. But in its rejection of reason, sentimentalism remains trapped within those feelings. In rejecting reason it rejects the key that unlocks the prison house of sentiment and opens wide the door of reality. Reason is panoramic, feeling is circumscribed.

We have ears and there happens to be sound. We have eyes and there happens to be color. We have lungs and there happens to be air. We have hunger and there happens to be food. There is a French aphorism stating that the best proof for the existence of water is the existence of thirst (*le preuve le plus croyable de l'existence de l'eau est l'existence de soif*). Consequently, the human desire for perfect justice, abiding peace, lasting happiness, and other intangibles also implies the existence of their proper object, which is God.

Johann Wolfgang von Goethe, who was a naturalist as well as a philosopher, remarked, "I do not doubt that there is life in the hereafter because it is in the order of nature that an entelechy cannot disappear." "Entelechy," a word derived from Aristotle, refers to the "end" (*telos*) for which each agent is inclined by nature. For Aristotle, the end is just as real as the beginning, an insight that was affirmed by Saint Thomas Aquinas. The desires we have for justice, peace, and happiness, are undeniable. But the longing for them that stirs our souls would never have been present without the existence of their corresponding objects of fulfillment. God is the ultimate object of our inborn desire for perfection, a perfection that we cannot find in this world.

When Pascal stated: "I would not have sought Him had I not already found Him," he was re-stating the Aristotelian position and applying it directly to God. How could anyone have the urge to look for something that does not exist? The existence of God is like a pulley that draws human beings to Him. That urge was placed in the heart of man by God Himself.

The religious impulse gets short circuited when it is stymied at the level of sentimentality. The world in which we inhabit may not be the one we would have created if we had the power to do so. Yet, as finite beings, we are in no position to question that which transcends our capabilities. God may be inscrutable but He has not abandoned us. He has left His mark on our souls. Our duty is to utilize that mark and understand how it leads back to Him.

Matthew Arnold's *Dover Beach* parallels Khayyam's fatalism when he centers two lovers in the context of an insane world:

Ah, love, let us be true
To one another! for the world, which seems
To lie before us like a land of dreams,
So various, so beautiful, so new,

Hath really neither joy, nor love, nor light,
Nor certitude, nor peace, nor help for pain;
And we are here as on a darkling plain
Swept with confused alarms of struggle and flight,
Where ignorant armies clash by night.

Here, again, is a very beautiful poem that evokes a strong sentiment. Yet, it is godless and offers no hope.

Poetry justifies itself by describing in a rich and imaginative way even things that are hopeless. Philosophy, on the other hand, has the burden of leading us to wisdom. Yet poetry can be seductive in that it can satisfy us on the level of feeling without urging us on to something higher. Our feelings are immediate. Philosophy is a journey. Nonetheless, we do not want to be locked in the enchantment of feeling. We must awaken and follow the signs that God has provided so that we can journey back to Him.

SOCIETY

We now live in a time which is called "The Post-Truth Era". While some people regard this as progressive and an enlargement of freedom, it is actually regressive and enslaving. Democracy requires the right combination of unity and diversity. People are diverse in many ways. Democracy honors that diversity by uniting its citizens on the basis of their fundamental equality and their God-given rights to life and liberty. Diversity itself, which welcomes contradictory elements, is an enemy of democracy.

Communism rejects the supreme importance of the individual; *laissez faire* capitalism rejects the importance of one's fellow citizen. Democracy rests on the harmony between an individual person's innate value and his obligation to contribute to society. It is the essential responsibility of political leaders to ensure that this balance is maintained. Unfortunately, we witness an appalling lack of leadership. Politicians seeking their own ends are currently widening the divide that separates citizens from each other. Discouragement, desperation and violence, rather than unity and peace, prevail. Materialism distracts consumers from their more important spiritual obligations.

Problems also exist on the level of education where political correctness speaks louder than the Sermon on the Mount.

Added to all these difficulties that block the path to democracy is the pandemic which, inevitably, intensifies one's concern for himself. Fear of contracting the Covid-19 virus along with economic hardships make it difficult for people to think of loftier things such as a true democracy of shared values.

The Mass Media, which subsidizes materialism through advertising, is not furthering the cause of democracy. Rather, it panders to left-wing values, particularly abortion. The liberal dream is for everyone to accept abortion. This impulse is

essentially totalitarian inasmuch as it rejects the legitimacy of the pro-life position and therefore wants to create a society in which defenders of life are systematically excluded.

What is critically needed at this hour is a revitalization of Christianity. Although Christianity is presently under attack, it contains precisely what is need for the restoration of democracy: love of neighbor, philosophical realism, reverence for what is good, respect for the beautiful, and a prayerful relationship with God.

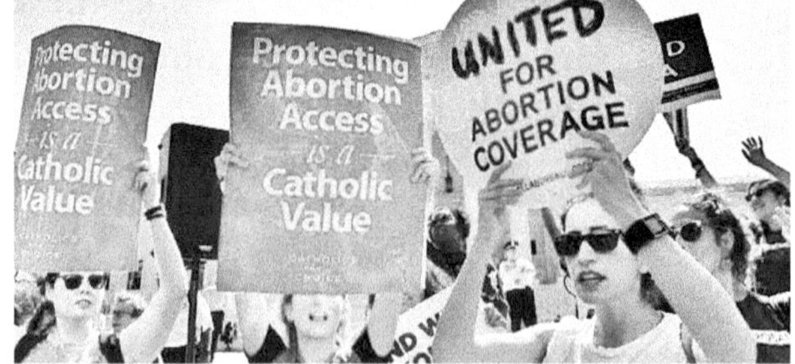

Democracy in the Post-Truth Era

Some secular journalists are now identifying our contemporary world as the "Post-Truth Era". This description is not simply hyperbole, but it does point to a condition that has many people concerned. Not every sector of society, of course, warrants this appellation. In sports, in law, and in science, for example, truth is irreplaceable. Baseball umpires are solemnly obliged to "get the call right". If there is any doubt about their judgment, it is subject to review. The obligation of judges and jurors is to come to the right verdict, a term composed of the Latin words *verum* and *dicere*, meaning to tell the truth. The collective aim of scientists is to uncover the truth of things, even though their efforts, despite a rigorous methodology, may continually approach truth but fall short of its ultimate revelation.

The two areas in which the term "Post-Truth" applies are education and the major media. Professor Allan Bloom's original title for his best-selling book, *The Closing of the American Mind* was somewhat longwinded, but most revealing: *How Higher Education Has Failed Democracy and Impoverished the Souls of Today's Students.* Bloom adverts to the problem in his very first sentence when he declares that:

> There is one thing a professor can be absolutely certain of: almost every student entering the university believes, or says he believes, that truth is relative.

Christopher Derrick is on the same page with Bloom. In his book, *Escape from Scepticism: Liberal Education as if Truth*

Mattered, he observes that:

> "Reality", "truth": on many a campus, these corny old words, would provoke an ironically sceptical raising of eyebrows.

Umpires, judges, and scientists must hold to truth as their guiding star. University students, however, are given a freedom that allows them to question tradition and pose solutions that are completely impractical.

Saint Thomas Aquinas' definition of truth is a model of simplicity: "The correspondence between the object and the intellect (*adequatio rei et intellectus*)." The Mass Media interposes itself between the intellect and its natural object so that "fake news" can replace reality. Instead of conforming to the real object, the mind conforms to whatever ideology the Media presents to it. Fake news is readily accepted when it confirms a pre-existing bias. In the words of Massimo Maoret, of the University of Navarra:

> in the age of post-truth, where intuitive emotion has replaced objective reasoning—many users [of social media] now lack the necessary critical thinking skills to distinguish between truth and fiction.

For many, transgenderism, the blurring of the sexes, same-sex marriage, pornography, and abortion are deemed acceptable simply because the Mass Media endorses them. For Dietrich von Hildebrand:

> One of the most ominous feature of the present epoch is undoubtedly the dethronement of truth.

Democracy thrives on truth. In the absence of truth, society drifts toward totalitarianism. The truth informs us of what is good and deserving of our commitment. Inevitably, in a post-truth world, censorship must play an important role in order to conceal truth from the masses. Amazon, a $1.5 trillion company has decided to ban books that allegedly contain "hate speech". Since hate-speech is undefined, it can be applied a range of attitudes. Ryan Anderson is the president of the prestigious Ethics and Public Policy Center in Washington, D.C. . Amazon has banned his book, *When Harry Became Sally: Responding to the Transgender Moment*, for reasons that are suspiciously ideological. The author, concerned about the truth of things, presents the case that the movement is motivated by a dubious ideology rather than on sound medical advice. Can the truth be an object of hate?

According to the new ideology, the two sexes are no longer distinctive, but interchangeable. Nonetheless, no one truly believes this. A Conservative MP in Canada is promoting *Bill C-233* which would ban sex-selective abortions. In this case, the sex of the child in the womb is clearly identifiable. It seems odd that a child's sex is determinable when it is in the womb, but not after it is born when the sex characteristics are more fully developed.

Because of the movement to abolish anything that does not fit into the current ideology, no author is safe, not even the Bard of Avon. An article in the *School Library Journal*, reports than many English teachers want Shakespeare removed from the curriculum. They want to "make room for modern, diverse, and inclusive voices". It is as if they are saying, "We want to be more inclusive, therefore, Shakespeare must be excluded; we want to be more diverse, so there is no room for the greatest playwright and poet in the English language". Shakespeare's plays have been translated into more than 100 languages and have been performed in at least 24 countries. He has survived the test of time because his message has universal validity and relates to the nature of the human being. The current moment, which is divided, confused, and at a critical crossroad, can hardly justify a claim to be the model for all cultures. Without the nourishing wisdom of the past, today's culture will soon be antiquated by the succeeding one.

Truth cannot be entirely suppressed. It continues to manifest itself to embarrass the lie. On certain college campuses today, there is an attempt to avoid "micro-aggressions". An example of this offense would be saying, "God bless you" to a person who may be an atheist. The horrors of abortion in which a child in the womb is killed, for many college students does not qualify to be classified as a micro-aggression. Christ's mandate to love one another is routinely rejected, along with the Church He founded because it could be offensive to non-Christians. It is unrealistic in the highest degree to think that a better world would emerge as a direct result of people avoiding micro-aggressions. The more likely result would be collective silence.

Democracy will be protected and strengthened by truth and tradition. The current trend toward arbitrary ideologies and "cancel culture" will be its ruination.

Giving Thanks to the Pilgrims

I grew up in Eastern Massachusetts, close enough to Plymouth Rock so that our family could travel to that historic spot, pay our respect, and get back home in time for supper. The legacy of the voyage of those stout-hearted pilgrims takes on special importance this year as we recall and celebrate that momentous event which took place exactly four hundred years ago.

The crossing of the Atlantic did not go according to plans. Originally, the pilgrims hoped to reach America in early October of 1620 using two ships. Delays and various complications, however, meant that they could use but one ship, the Mayflower. Their intended destination was the Colony of Virginia. Storms blew them off course, north to the hook of Cape Cod. The food supply was running low and it was not prudent to sail southward to arrive at their original destination.

Some of the non-Puritans on board threatened a rebellion since their newly discovered territory had no laws to hold society in place. They "would use their own liberty; for none had power to command them". The situation was critical. In order to avoid mayhem, the pilgrims decided to establish their own government. Thus, they drew up the *Mayflower Compact*, which was duly signed by 41 of the male members aboard ship. It served as a social contract binding the settlers to follow community rules and regulations for the good of all.

The pilgrims, therefore, pledged to:

> combine ourselves together into a civill body politick, for our better ordering and preservation, and furtherance of the ends aforesaid; and by virtue hereof to enacte, constitute, and frame such just and equall laws, ordinances, acts, constitutions and offices, from time to time, as shall be thought most meete and convenient for the generall good of the Colonie unto which we promise all due submission and obedience.

Although conceived and executed under unexpected and impromptu circumstances, the *Mayflower Compact* is of great historical importance. In 1920, the tercentenary of the landing at Plymouth, Calvin Coolidge, put the signing of the Compact in historical perspective:

> The compact which they signed was an event of the greatest importance. It was the foundation of liberty based on law and order, and that tradition has been steadily upheld. They drew up a form of government which has been designated as the first real constitution of modern times. It was democratic, an acknowledgment of liberty under law and order and the giving to each person the right to participate in the government, while they promised to be obedient to the laws.

There were 102 pilgrims who set sail for America on the Mayflower. A certain William Butten died in a storm just three days before land was sighted. A boy was born during the ten week sojourn and was appropriately named Oceanus (surname, Hopkins). Statisticians reckon that about ten million Americans should be able to trace their ancestry back to the Mayflower. The count was not as significant as the strong Christian faith and respect for law and order that the pilgrims brought to the new land.

Piety is a lost virtue. One might even say, in the light of recent events, that it is now regarded as a vice. Piety is the respect that is owed to our ancestors, to tradition, to all the things for which we should offer thanks. G. K. Chesterton reminds us that "Tradition does not mean that the living are dead but that the dead are alive." In February of this year, a 17-year-old high schooler was charged with 11 felony accounts of vandalism to property. The charges stem from a Feb. 17 vandalism spree that targeted the Plymouth Rock, Forefathers Monument and

several other landmarks and attractions along the downtown Plymouth waterfront. Plymouth Rock has been consistent target over the years, for people who have a political agenda. Now visitors to Plymouth Rock may see it spray painted with graffiti and be dismayed.

The *Mayflower Compact* was signed by 41 men and no women. To the contemporary mind that is infected with extreme self-righteousness, this is intolerable and should negate whatever value or virtues may be associated with our pilgrim fathers. 1620 was four hundred years ago. At that time there was a clear distinction between men and women, one that should be a model for today's world that has blurred the distinction and abuses anyone who believes that God made them male and female. It was a distinction that did not alienate the sexes, but complemented them so that they could work together and remain married together. Our thanks should go to the pilgrims to whom we are deeply indebted and certainly not to those irreverent iconoclasts who seem incapable of offering thanks to anyone.

In response to the vandalism, Lea Filson, executive director of the tourism group See Plymouth announced that she was "heartsick". "This is the first place families arrived in the New World to begin a colony," she said. "This is the only example of Native peoples and English colonists to agree to a peace alliance and keep it for over half a century." Lea Filson, herself, is a descendent of pilgrims who arrived on the Mayflower.

William Fahey is the President of Thomas More College of Liberal Arts in New Hampshire. I like the way he has placed today's Thanksgiving in the proper perspective focusing on what is essential to the feast day:

> The day is richer than drumsticks and drink and a paid holiday off. Let those things remain, but let them become prompts for our recollection and our gratitude. For another has paid for the feast.

LOVE AND SUCCESS

A politician charms his voters by promising them better opportunities for success. Christ, on the other hand, is not at all concerned about success. He demands that all people love each other. Love is not necessarily a path to success. Christ, Himself, crucified at 33 among thieves, was not, in the eyes of the world, a success.

The politician promises to make things better on the outside. Christ is concerned about who we are on the inside. Success, as the world understands it, is defined in material terms. Fame, fortune, social status, a fine car, a fashionable wardrobe, and a fine house are success's emblems. But this portrait of the successful person is not the portrait of saints.

Christ's mandate could not be more clear: "What does it profit a man if he shall gain the whole world and loses his own his soul?"(Mark 8:36). "It is easier for a camel to pass through the eye of the needle than a rich man to enter the kingdom of God" (Matthew 19:24). "If you want to be perfect, go, sell your possessions and give to the poor, and you will have treasure in heaven. Then come, follow Me" (Luke 12:33).

The politician promises things that are both impossible and unfulfilling. The notion of equal opportunities for all is sheer nonsense. Our opportunities are limited by our genetic endowment. A blind man cannot be an umpire. A deaf person cannot become a symphony conductor. Moreover, opportunity is a morally neutral term. It is not a good in itself. The Internet has created opportunities for thieves and hackers to pilfer assets and create mayhem.

We should be more concerned about obligation than opportunity. We have one fundamental obligation: to love self, neighbor and God. Opportunities are like buses, there is always another one that will come along. Politicians are concerned about structural changes that create new opportunities for success. The Christian is more interested in personal growth which may or may not coincide with worldly success.

It is important to note that obligation, in the sense that we are describing it here, is related to truth. Only when there is a relationship to truth is an obligation genuine. Improved opportunities will be of little benefit to people if they are not anchored in truth and thereby, correspond to doing what is good. In his encyclical, *Centesimus Annus*, Pope St. John Paul II expressed his concern that material success could obscure the more prior consideration of personal growth:

> In the developed countries there is sometimes an excessive promotion of purely utilitarian values, with an appeal to the appetites and inclinations towards immediate gratification, making it difficult to recognize and respect the hierarchy of the true values of human existence (29).

During the Covid-19 pandemic, most Americans, because of severe restrictions, are experiencing the loss of a great deal of opportunities. Dining in restaurants, social gatherings, weddings, funerals, and so on, have been greatly curtailed. Businesses have been shut down and, in some cases, churches have been closed. Whereas opportunities have been evaporating, the obligations to love and to grow as a person remain intact. The loss of economic and social opportunities does not translate into the loss of one's fundamental obligation to love.

It is both sad as well as disconcerting that many people, being dependent on material comforts and opportunities, have turned to self-destructive forms of behavior. Depression, alcoholism, drug addiction have claimed many lives. The current pandemic, horrific as it is, nonetheless offers the challenge to summon, as philosopher/theologian Paul Tillich has expressed it, *The Courage To Be.*

For Tillich and many other contemporary thinkers, the prevailing anxiety of the modern world is "meaninglessness". Life, however, is not inherently meaningless. Nonetheless, if we build a house of cards based on momentary pleasures and material possessions, (while ignoring the development of our own personhood), that paper-mache edifice will certainly crumble. The consequence is a sense of emptiness that leads to utter meaninglessness. Sigmund Freud, despite his many dubious declarations, was on the mark when he stated that material wealth does not bring happiness to a person because it does not correspond to an infantile wish. Our most basic need, which perdures throughout our lifetime, is not for possessions, but for the giving and receiving of love.

A rather insidious problem occurs while people are quarantined. Inevitably, they watch television on a more extended basis and are bombarded with endless images of attractive material possessions brought to their attention through the mass media. In the current crisis, authentic education is of far greater need than digesting commercial advertisements. Like the mythical Tantalus, people are tempted to lust for what is just out of their reach.

As Pope John II stated in *Centesimus Annus*:

> Thus a great deal of educational work is urgently needed including the education of consumers in the responsible use of choice, the formation of a strong sense of responsibility among producers and among people in the mass media in particular, as well as the necessary intervention by public authorities (36).

We do not mean to criticize politicians for creating opportunities. Politicians have a legitimate and noble role to play. What we are concerned about here is too heavy a reliance on material things—the sweet siren call of success—accompanied by a neglect of the role that love plays in the development of the whole person.

Politicians, in order to remain in office, must be elected by the majority. Their office is temporary. Christ does not run for election. His term is forever. But He must be chosen by each individual person through love. And that is the great blessing and advantage He brings to our lives.

THOUGHT AND ACTION

A physicist friend of mine told me that one of his students wanted to become a physicist but hated mathematics. My colleague laughed at contradiction. This odd separation of ends from their indispensable means is, however, not all that unusual. All my students, for example, want to be happy, but a rather small percentage of them a willing to accept the means necessary to attain that desirable end. Here is one of the great paradoxes of life: the concrete stands on the shoulders of the abstract. Therefore, it is so easy for students to separate them from each other, the former being evident and tangible, while the latter remains hidden and intangible. Nonetheless, as reason tells us, an unseen God created the visible world. Can we deny the Creator his existence?

This separation of ends from their means can be associated with a similar separation of action from thought. It is all too common for people, seeing little value in philosophy, to deplore certain actions while remaining indifferent to the very thoughts upon which they rely. This is a most serious problem since philosophy gives us the enlightenment we need in order to prevent the emergence of deplorable actions. Philosophy, though intangible, is extremely practical when it is properly applied.

I am utterly fascinated, therefore, by how people can protest against certain actions without protesting against the very ideas that contribute directly to those actions. The example of Dietrich von Hildebrand and his wife, Alice, well illustrates the point. Dietrich had both the intelligence and the courage to speak out against Hitler and Nazism. His strong and well circulated objections earned him the distinction of being the number one enemy of the third Reich. A warrant was issued for his assassination. Through the assistance of many friends, he fled to Austria, then to France, to Portugal, to Brazil, and finally to the United States where he began a teaching career in the philosophy department at Fordham University. According to his wife:

> My husband's ardent love for truth is what allowed him to perceive the poison of the Nazi philosophy so quickly. When truth was violated, it registered clearly to someone who had such an appreciation for it.

Von Hildebrand's philosophy is essentially anti-Nazi. Moreover, the root of his philosophy lies in the fundamental value of truth. In a chapter entitled "*The Dethronement of Truth*," in his book, *The Tower of Babel* (1953), he refers to the Bavarian minister of education, a certain Hans Schemm, who made the following astonishing statement before an assembly of university professors:

> From this day on, you will no longer have to examine whether something is true or not, but exclusively whether or not it corresponds to the Nazi ideology.

In this way, no one has any basis from which he can denounce Nazism. An ideology without a justifying philosophy is something that any intelligent person should reject. It is truth that determines whether a position is right or wrong, and certainly not the biased sentiments of the Nordic race. Dethrone truth and war becomes inevitable. Von Hildebrand records his courageous stand in his book, *My Battle Against Hitler: Faith, Truth and Defiance in the Shadow of the Third Reich.*

Von Hildebrand's wife, Alice, brought her husband's anti-Nazi philosophy to Hunter College, where she taught philosophy for 37 years. In her autobiography, *Memoirs of a Happy Failure* (2014), she recounts how she was persecuted for disagreeing with the dominant school of relativism. Harvard law professor, Mary Ann Glendon, attests that "Her love of truth shines forth on every page of this fascinating personal memoir". But her commitment to truth was her greatest obstacle. In fact, she was told by her school administrators not to teach objective truth. It took 15 years for Hunter College just to give Alice her own desk. "Someone – God – wanted me there," she writes. "After 13 years I was granted tenure," she recalls, by a 9 to 8 vote, passing an unprecedented Gestapo-like interview of two hours by 15 heads of departments and two deans. She and others as well regarded her being awarded tenure as a "miracle". Not everyone shared this view, however. Astonishingly, even rabbis, several of them in fact, protested against her being granted tenure. "In secular universities" as Alice observes, "the word 'objective truth' triggers panic."

How can it be that Nazism is universally denounced, while the very ideas that spawned it not only remain free from criticism but those who bring it to light are censured? Relativism produces an atmosphere in which ideologies like Nazism thrive. The answer may be complex, but surely one of the key factors is a separation of thought from action, means from ends, cause from effect, or philosophy from life. Alice von Hildebrand, like her distinguished husband, was a philosopher. For this she paid the price. But she also reaped the harvest, particularly in the joy of knowing that her teaching inspired and guided many of her students into the Catholic Church. In 2013, Pope Francis formally recognized her as a Dame Grand Cross of the Equestrian Order of St. Gregory in recognition of her lifetime of work on behalf of the Church.

Alice von Hildebrand and her husband Dietrich devoted their lives to a philosophy that rested on three pillars: **reverence, value,** and **God**. When we have reverence for the natural values of life, including human life itself, we are moving in the direction of God who created all things that are good and thereby inscribed with value. In her biography of her late husband, *The Soul of a Lion* (2000), which resonates with their shared philosophy, including their mutual opposition to abortion, she records his final words: "A country that legalizes murder is doomed." If abortion is the dethronement of truth, then we are surely doomed.

Equality and the Tenth Commandment

The tenth Commandment reads: "Thou shall not covet thy neighbor's goods". This commandment is rich in implication. First of all, it applies to all of us equally. We are all equal in the eyes of God as moral beings. No one is exempt from the moral order. The word "covet" is synonymous with the more familiar term, "envy". We are strongly advised, therefore, not to envy what our neighbor has that we may lack. Envy is a Deadly Sin. It is, as the historical record shows, a disposition that can lead to anger, violence, and warfare. It is a vice that can spawn other vices.

Envy distracts us from virtues that we should put into practice, such as industry, responsibility, motivation, and gratitude for what we have. It is far better to improve ourselves rather than envy others. Envy creates a mood of discontent and contains an element of injustice, especially when what is coveted rightfully belongs to our neighbor. The Judaeo-Christian position encourages self-development, but it also encourages counting our blessings.

The Tenth Commandment has been criticized inasmuch

as it accepts the inequality of goods that pertains between the "haves" and the "have-nots". This inequality may be remedied by social justice that is motivated by charity. It need not be a permanent situation. The Christian position is to avoid envy, develop one's self as a person and work for the common good.

The Marxist-Communist position is to utilize envy as the engine that ignites a revolution. The end result of the revolution, theoretically, is for the State to establish equality of goods for everyone. Thus, envy is seen, in the communist perspective, as a virtue that leads, through violence if necessary, to a universal equality of possessions. In practice, however, this theory has never achieved what the revolution had promised, though untold millions have died in the aborted attempt.

The term "equality" has a broad range of application. The Declaration of Independence states that "all men are created equal". The *Preamble of the United States Constitution* refers to "We the people of the United States". By contrast, the Marxist-Communist view is one that denies both God and creation, while referring to the "people" and the "masses". What communism hopes to achieve through a State enforced equality of goods, it loses in relation to the individual nature of each human being. According to Karl Marx, "the individual, of and by himself, has no value unless he is a member of the revolutionary mass". Therefore, man exists for the State, rather than the State existing for man.

Saint John Paul II's major contribution as a philosopher is his careful articulation of the human being as a person. Accordingly, a person is a dynamic integration of unique individuality and communal responsibility. Each human being, then, is both equal as a human being and unequal in terms of his unique identity. For Marx, Lenin, and Stalin, the individual person has no value in himself, but wholly subordinated to the State. For Marx, "Communism begins where atheism begins . . . We can create a new man if we confiscate all property and if we persecute religion".

Communism rejects the worth of the individual person. Christianity holds that each individual person is created in the image and likeness of God. On this point these two systems of thought could hardly be further apart. Pope Pius, XI, therefore, could be justified in stating the following in his encyclical, *Divini Redemptoris* (1937):

> Venerable Brethren, see that the faithful are put on guard against these deceitful methods. Communism is intrinsically evil, and therefore no one who desires to save Christian civilization from extinction should render it assistance in any enterprise whatsoever.

Fedor Dostoevsky understood with extraordinary clarity the radical incompatibility between Communism and Christianity. Communism denied the worth of the individual person and placed him at the mercy of the State. Dostoevsky was correct in stating that "Our people are not only becoming atheists, but believe in atheism as if it were a religion". Communism of the Marx, Lenin, Stalin variety is omnivorous. It is totalitarian in its essence and not a party. As Vyacheslav Molotov, a leading figure in the Soviet government observed, "Communism is in power; all the other parties are in jail".

In America, at the moment, there is a noticeable love affair with socialism. The notion of equality is mesmerizing, even if it is the kind that robs the human being of his unique identity. We would be wise, however, to take seriously Christopher Dawson's warning that "socialism is a half-way house to communism". We are different in many ways, both by nature and by achievement. These differences should not cause us to envy one another. Nor should it precipitate a strong socialist government. If a Christian revolution is needed, it is a revolution of love. Love honors and embraces differences. It is the inspiration that puts into practice the corporal works of mercy: feeding the hungry, giving drink to the thirsty, clothing the naked, providing shelter for the homeless, visiting the sick and the imprisoned, and finally, burying the dead. Christianity differs from atheistic communism as mercy differs from violence.

The Tenth Commandment is not purely negative. In condemning envy, it implies living a life of virtue, one that promotes the good of the person and at the same time, the good of others. Marxist/Communism does not believe in love or virtue; it believes in force. Democracy will succeed only when people are virtuous. As people drift away from virtue, they become attracted to the power of the State. The Tenth Commandment gives us fair warning.

HUMANITY

The human being is a most mysterious and perplexing character. On the one hand, he is viewed as created in the image and likeness of God. On the other hand, he is regarded as a cosmic accident, a being who has neither value nor meaning. The inscription on the forecourt of the Temple of Apollo at Delphi, "Know thyself," has retained its enduring importance. "Who am I?" is the question that each person puts to himself and never receives a fully satisfactory answer.

Pride makes us think that we are more important than we really are, while self-abasement lowers our estimation of our true self. Humility is the virtue that allows us to gain a realistic appraisal of our self, not too lofty and not to lamentable.

Philosophers such as Josef Pieper, Jacques Maritain, Etienne Gilson, and Saint John Paul II have taken pains to portray the human being realistically. Accordingly, a human being is mortal, fallible, engendered, solitary, and communal. He is a knowing, loving, creative, and God-fearing being whose life has both meaning and purpose. He grows as a person through virtue. The Seven Deadly Sins are his ruination. In a word, for these philosophers, he is a "person". Hence, their philosophy is one of "personalism".

Ignorance of self, however, haunts people. They often settle for an image of themselves, as did Narcissus. This image may represent fame, wealth, success, status, or popularity. Possessions, awards, accolades, and trophies, then, are re-

garded as more important than simply being a good person. The highly acclaimed motion picture, *Citizen Kane*, dramatically illustrates how unsatisfactory it is to attach the meaning of

one's life to fame and fortune. External ornaments never satisfy the needs of the heart. At the same time, we can accomplish extraordinary things by simply being ourselves.

We are made to love and be loved. Peace of mind will continue to elude us as long as we try to achieve something for which we have no innate aptitude. The dictum "Know thyself" should be followed by "Be Thyself". God does not ask of us the impossible.

What Does It Mean To Be Human?

It is all too common, when a person makes a mistake, to excuse him by saying, "Well, he is only human". "Only human" implies a nature that is fundamentally irredeemable. It disregards man's true nature that is reflected in the "humanities" which celebrate the highpoints in human actions and achievements. Philosopher Gabriel Marcel, after hearing a Johann Sebastian Bach concert, tells us that he experienced a revival of a certainty that seems to be lost in the modern world: "the honor of being a human". To be truly human is to exemplify the best of man's nature. We need these experiences so that we do not despair and begin to think that a human being is a degenerate animal who is at home in sin.

A journalist for the *Toronto Star* offers us a clear example of the view that the human being is essentially degenerate. In an article entitled, "It's the sinning that makes us human," he maintains that "Sin is us". "Indeed," as he contends, "it helps to define us and make us human". It is true, we may concede, that, from an historical point of view, man has a spotty track record; but, that is because he keeps falling short of his real self. Gerard Manley Hopkins fully acknowledges the weaknesses of the human being, but also acknowledges the glory of his essence. He concludes his poem, *That Nature is a Heraclitean Fire*, by completing the paradox:

This Jack, joke, poor potsherd, | patch, matchwood, immortal diamond.

Is immortal diamond.

We are, all of us, "immortal diamonds" made in the image and likeness of God. If we could only realize that and live accordingly. The Seven Deadly Sins do not define us; they warn us about the ways in which we can descend into our lower selves.

Our Canadian journalist goes through the Seven Deadly Sins in a rather desperate attempt to convince his readers that they characterize our humanity. "Virtue, on the other hand," he warns, "is what keeps us from being human". Vice is nice; but virtue can hurt you. What is pride, our journalist informs us, but "self-respect"? We can be proud of our achievements, our possessions, and anything that enhances our self-image. Friedrich Nietzsche is the great apostle of pride. The "Will to Power" is his personal motto. Envy is "motivation". Certainly Karl Marx agreed with this, since it galvanized the proletariat to start a revolution. Anger is "righteous indignation". Even Christ showed anger at the money merchants. Who would not be moved to anger when he is a victim of injustice? Lust is simply biology. Here, our writer would find support in the thinking of Sigmund Freud and many others who find lust to be a moral imperative. It is, as Malcolm Muggeridge has stated, the "mysticism of materialism" for the modern world. Sloth is "nature's way of telling us to slow down". Medical science warns us about the Type A personality that is hyperactive and self-destructive. We are well advised to take it easy. Gluttony and greed are omitted from our journalist's analysis, but it is easy, given his slant on the Deadly Sins, how they could be misdiagnosed as virtues. Gluttony, presumably, is simply natural. Bar owners throughout the world could attest to this. As for greed, we can hand the baton over to Gordon Gecko, played by Michael Douglas in the notion picture, *Wall Street*:

> Greed is right. Greed works. Greed clarifies, cuts through and captures the essence of the evolutionary spirit. Greed in all of its forms—greed for life, for money, for love, knowledge—has marked the upward surge of mankind . . .

Language can be slippery. If we want to distinguish virtue from vice, we must be sensitive to the various shades of meaning that a particular word can assume. We can take justifiable pride in something related to us that is good. We can be proud of our family, our friends, and country, and our Church. Pride is a vice when the self seeks inordinate praise. Vainglory, boasting, inordinate ambition, and hypocrisy are obviously not virtues. They epitomize pride as a deadly sin. Envy is sorrow over another's good fortune. It is essentially anti-social and self-deprecating. We should take joy in another's good fortune, especially when that fortune is justified. Anger is a vice when it is excessive. As such, it can lead to various forms of vengeance, including murder. Lust looks at the person, not as a person, but as a sex object. Lust is certainly not love, which seeks the good of the person. Sloth is not laziness, as it is commonly thought. It is the reluctance or the refusal to take delight in spiritual things. The slothful person disdains prayer, religious practices, good music, reading, and study. Gluttony represents an inordinate desire for the pleasures the table. It is a vice that can lead to addiction and, therefore, can be self-destructive. Finally, greed, often referred to as "avarice" is an inordinate desire for material things. It contains the element of selfishness and can be an impediment with regard to social justice.

Virtue is perfective of the person. Vice is ruinous. In order to recognize virtue as a true reality that is perfective of the person, we need to use our capacity for reason. Thus, Joseph Pieper in his book, *The Four Cardinal Virtues*, can state, citing St. Thomas Aquinas, that:

> The intrinsic goodness of man—and that is the same as saying his true humanness—consists in this, that 'reason perfected in the cognition of truth' shall inwardly shape and imprint his volition and actions.

A life of virtue reveals the glory of man.

Leadership in a Time of Crisis

The present crisis in America is broad and deep. The Covid-19 pandemic has further exacerbated an existing crisis in which politics, morality, and religion are divided to the point that dialogue no longer seems possible. There seems little hope for a solution from within. Political parties, ethicists, and the clergy are at war with each other. Can there be a solution from the outside, above the fray?

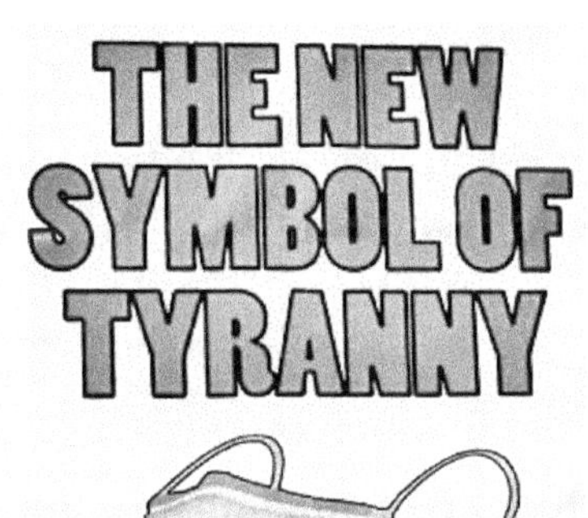

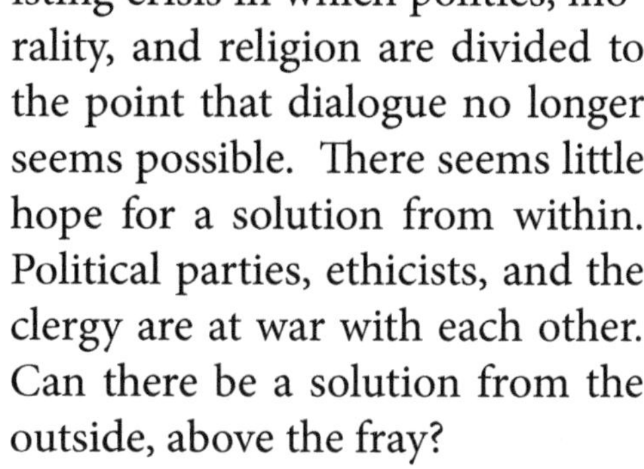

Politics is inveighing against religion. *The New Yorker* has boldly predicted that President Biden may "save American Catholicism from the far right". Bishops are fighting bishops. The Vatican seems to be spreading confusion. The government is crushing the freedom to worship. Morality remains in the never-never land of relativism. Men and women are no longer men and women. Pandemic experts have received death threats. Philosophy appears to be both archaic and irrelevant. We now live under an established state, what political commentator John O'Sullivan has described as an "odd syncretic blend of paganism, sexual polyversity, and scientism." What is critically needed is leadership, a word that inspires hope but remains elusive.

Mortimer Adler was America's premier educator and philosopher. Following Aristotle, he taught that leadership is comprised of three factors: *ethos, pathos,* and *logos.* With regard to a good leader, ***ethos*** refers to his moral character, which would include courage, rectitude, and determination. ***Pathos*** refers to his ability to touch people emotionally. ***Logos*** is his ability to give solid reasons for his thoughts and actions, to be able to move people intellectually. It may be rare to find all three of these factors in the same person, but so is true leadership.

If the type of leader that Aristotle and Adler outline does not seem readily available, it is nonetheless important to understand what true leadership is so that potential leaders can aspire to the role. It is also helpful to learn of great leaders of the past who were able to answer a crisis. We may think of Washington, Lincoln, FDR, Churchill, Pope Pius XII, and Saint John Paul II. Yet these heroic figures were not called to deal with a plague.

Let us recall to mind Saint Charles Borromeo, a heroic leader who responded to the challenges of the plague that broke out in Milan, Italy in the year 1577. St. Charles was out of town when the plague began, but hastened back to Milan to inspire confidence in his beleaguered citizens. He was convinced that God had sent the plague as a chastisement for sin. Therefore, he sought all the more to give himself over to prayer.

He prepared himself for death, made out his will, and gave himself entirely to his people. He made personal visits to plague stricken homes and to hospitals where the worst cases were to be found. It was at this time that this courageous bishop walked in procession, barefooted, with a thick penitential cord around his neck, at one time bearing in his hand the relic of the Holy Nail. His example and his actions proved effective as a powerful Christian witness for many of his fellow citizens. St. Charles later wrote his *Memoriale* recalling the lessons given by the cessation of the plague.

The parallels between the plague that ravaged northern Italy in the 16th century and the current situation in the United States are striking. Will another Charles Borromeo emerge to provide the courage and leadership needed to bring people back to God? Presently Americans seem to be relying more than they should on politics and science and less than they should on prayer and fasting.

Why Josef Pieper Needs To Be Read

There are two ironies that characterize the life and works of Josef Pieper. He was born in the year 1904 in the Westphalian village of Elte, a town so isolated that no train was available to take any of its citizens to any other part of Westphalia. Yet Pieper's many books, in many translations, are well traveled and are read throughout the world. Secondly, though his philosophy is rooted in a 13th century thinker—Saint Thomas Aquinas—it is most timely. Speaking of his "hero," he stated that the work of Aquinas "is inexhaustible and his affirmative way of looking at the reality of the whole creation seems to me a necessary correction modern Christianity cannot do without".

Pieper passed away in 1997. His keen insight into modern liberalism, however, applies perfectly to the current crisis that reigns in 2021. In *Fortitude and Temperance* (1954), he writes:

> Enlightened liberalism, closes its eyes to the evil in the world: to the demonic power of 'our adversary' the Devil, the Evil One, as well as to the mysterious power of human delusion and perversion of will; at worst, the liberal imagines the power of evil to be not so "gravely" dangerous that

> one could not "negotiate" or "come to terms" with it. The uncomfortable, merciless and inexorable "No," a self-evident reality to the Christian, has been obliterated from the liberalistic world view.

Today's liberal believes that all man needs to prosper as a human being can be found in politics. In his view, politics replaces religion. He does not believe that he needs to overcome life's difficulties through virtue. To him, the ethical life unfolds "free from sorrow and harm". Liberalism and naiveté go hand in hand.

The "liberal" conception of man does not include virtues, which are man's moral life blood. Pieper, on the other hand, is perhaps most noted for his books on virtue, especially the cardinal virtues of Prudence, Justice, Fortitude and Temperance. In fact, he has come to be known as "The Philosopher of Virtue". "Surrender to sensuality," he warns in *The Four Cardinal Virtues*, "paralyzes the powers of the moral person". "Modern man," Pieper writes, "cannot conceive of a good act which might not be imprudent, nor of a bad act which might be prudent". Thus chastity, truthfulness, and courageous sacrifice appear to be imprudent, while lying, avarice, and ostentation appear to be prudent.

Prudence

We need to read the works of this eminent philosopher so that we can better understand what is happening in the present. In *The Silence of Saint Thomas*, he remarks that:

> the truth will be more profound as truth, the more vigorously its timeliness comes to light; it also means that a man experiencing his own time with a richer intensity of heart and fuller spiritual awareness has a better chance of experiencing the illuminating force of truth.

Pieper has a remarkable ability to restate traditional wisdom in terms of contemporary problems. This is well documented in *Belief and Faith*, *Happiness and Contemplation*, *The End of Time*, and *Guide to Thomas Aquinas*.

T. S. Eliot, who wrote the Introduction to Pieper's *Leisure the Basis of Culture*, pays the author high praise, crediting him with restoring to philosophy, "what common sense obstinately tells us ought to be found there: insight and wisdom". The late Ralph McInerny avers that:

> No one has written more wisely on the relation between thinking and doing than Pieper, yet there are no obstacles of erudition between the reader and the presentation.

Pieper is not only worth reading, he is also readable.

Justice

The eminent psychiatrist, Karl Stern, was a good friend of Pieper. In his collection of essays, *Love and Success*, Stern recalls being on a plane after attending a convention which was a strange mixture of half-understood existentialism, sociology, group dynamics, anthropology, and psychoanalysis. He recalls:

> Reading Pieper on my way home, I felt like someone who,

> with his ears still full of street noise, suddenly finds himself listening to *The Art of the Fugue*. I was back in a world of immutable harmony.

We should read the works of Josef Pieper because he opens the door to that perennial philosophy which is the love of wisdom. He makes Aquinas understandable, and whets our appetite for wisdom. As a lover of words, Pieper points out that the word for wise in Latin is *sapiens* while its cognate, *sapere*, is the word for taste. Wisdom is accessible to us, so much so that we can "taste" it. Pieper's philosophy may be summarized in a phrase by Bernard of Clairvaux: "A wise man is one who savors all things as they really are". "Taste and see that the Lord is Good" (Psalm 34:8).

Fortitude

Temperance

The Triumph of the Outcast

On January 22, 2021, a date of special significance for pro-lifers, legendary baseball player, Hank Aaron passed away peacefully in his sleep at the age of 86. Less known to the public than his impressive batting statistics was the strength he drew from his Catholic faith. In 1959, while he was playing with the Milwaukee Braves, Aaron and his family converted to Catholicism partly due to his friendship with an influential priest, Father Michael Sablica of the Milwaukee Archdiocese, an early pioneer for racial justice in Milwaukee. Aaron credited Father Sablica for helping him grow as a person in the 1950s when baseball often reflected the kind of prejudice and racism that was rampant in the South.

Hank was said to be a frequent reader of "The Imitation of Christ" by Thomas à Kempis, which he kept in his locker. He also kept a copy of Bishop Fulton Sheen's Catholic booklet, *The Life of Christ*, in his glove compartment. "I need to depend on Someone who is bigger, stronger, and wiser than I am," he said. "I don't do it on my own. God is my strength. He gave me a good bound and some talent and the freedom to develop it. He helps me when things go wrong. He forgives me when I fall on my face. He lights the way." Aaron, however, did not remain a Catholic throughout his life. He became a Baptist with his second marriage. His funeral service took place at the Friendship Baptist Church in Atlanta.

In his definitive autobiography, *I Had a Hammer*, Aaron recounts an incident in his father's life that, in retrospect, gives his own life a parabolic quality. It parallels the parable about the stone that the builders rejected which became a cornerstone (Psalm 118:22). It was 1928. Hank's dad, a gifted athlete in his own right, wanted to watch the great Sultan of Swat, Babe Ruth, who was playing in an exhibition game in Mobile, Alabama. Herbert Aaron was a poor black living in an environment where racial tensions were particularly intense. In order to witness the game, he climbed a tree that overlooked the park. He swore that he saw Ruth hit a homerun that landed into the coal car of a passing train. The ball was not retrieved until it arrived in New Orleans. As he watched from his precarious perch, like Zacchaeus from a tree (Luke 19:1-10), little could he have suspected or imagined that the day would come when his own son would break the Bambino's career homerun record.

On the night of April 8, 1974, the improbable became a reality. On that date – voted by baseball fans across the country as the most memorable event in baseball history — Herbert Aaron's son, who was born on the day before Ruth's 39th birthday, who wore number 44 and had hit exactly 44 home runs in 4 separate seasons, hit the first pitch thrown by Al Downing of the Los Angeles Dodgers into the left field bullpen for his 715th round-tripper thereby breaking Babe Ruth's seemingly unsurpassable record of 714. He was greeted at home plate by his father and his mother, Estella, who embraced him in her protective arms.

53,755 fans were in attendance that night in the Atlanta stadium while an estimated 35 million watched the event on television. Perhaps legendary announcer Vin Scully best captured the significance of the event in stating that:

> A black man is getting a standing ovation in the deep south for breaking a record of an all-time baseball idol. It is a great moment for all of us and particularly for Henry Aaron.

Putting Henry Louis Aaron's life in perspective, Georgia Gov. Brian Kemp said in a statement on behalf of the Aaron family, that "Hank Aaron was an American icon and one of Georgia's greatest legends. His life and career made history, and his influence was felt not only in the world of sports, but far beyond — through his important work to advance civil rights and create a more equal, just society. We ask all Georgians to join us in praying for his fans, family, and loved ones as we remember Hammerin' Hank's incredible legacy."

Henry Aaron was selected to the All Star Game 25 times. He won a Most Valuable Player Award, hit 20 or more homeruns 20 times, finished his career with major league records in runs batted in (2,229), total bases (6,856), and extra-base hits (1,477). He won 3 Golden Gloves and twice led the National League in batting average. The Lou Gehrig Memorial Award, the Presidential Medal of Freedom, and awards for his work in improving race relations are listed among his numerous off-the-field awards. Not bad for a person who, in his younger years, could not afford a bat or a ball and had to resort to hitting bottle caps with a stick.

All in all, this is a great story. Yet it is set in the context of an even greater story. Long ago in Bethlehem, a father was denied entrance at an inn. There was no room for him there. His Son, the King of Peace, far surpassing the wisdom of the poor innkeeper, ultimately broke all the barriers that keep social classes alienated from each other. It is the prototypic story of the outcast who turns out to be a bearer of the transcendent. We should not weep our outcast state, for it may be the first step to a great story.

All great stories are counter-cultural. And all great stories are usually best appreciated in retrospect. We are blinded by the moment and are unable to see what is slowly unfolding. But what are the great stories that are unfolding at the moment? What are the barriers that today's heroes are now unceremoniously crossing? What is the urgent message that the world now needs to hear? God and His providential care remains in control. We should live patiently and with hope.

Why We Love to Watch Team Sports

There are four basic ingredients to team sports that mirror the very same ingredients that are required for a good life. These basic ingredients are goal, order, skill, and cooperation. Every sport needs a goal: the football player desires the end zone, the hockey player seeks the net, the basketball player aims for the hoop, while the baseball player hopes to cross home plate. Collectively, each team wants to win. Secondly, order is clearly apparent on the gridiron, the red and blue lines on the surface of the hockey rink, the painted lines on the court, and the circuit that runs from first base to home. No athlete can long endure in his sport if he lacks the requisite skills. Finally, cooperation is essential, whether it be the assists in hockey, basketball and baseball or the sacrifices that the batter makes to advance a runner.

The fact that life is difficult whereas watching sports on TV is easy, gives spectating a huge advantage over participating. A glimpse of some of the astronomical salaries paid to professional athletes indicates the immense popularity and success

of team sports. Mookie Betts of the Los Angeles Dodgers, has a contract guaranteeing him $365 million over ten years. Giannis Antetokounpo has signed with the Milwaukee Bucks for $228.2 million for five years. Quarterback Tom Brady recently purchased a $2 million yacht which is a mere 1% of his estimated worth of $200 million. A Mickey Mantle rookie card has sold for $5.2 million, while a Wayne Gretzky rookie card netted $1.29 million. The Covid-depressed economy does not seem to have affected the stratospheric salaries of star players or lessened the enthusiasm of its fans.

The TV watcher allows no excuses for mishaps. He may fly into a rage over a fumble, penalty, foul, or error. Fred Snodgrass, Bill Buckner, "Wrong Way" Jim Marshall, Leon Lett, and Mickey Owen, to name just a few, have been immortalized in a Hall of Shame for making miscues at critical times. The viewer, however, may be a clever practitioner of excuses for his own failures. What is the goal of life? Do I invent my own goals? Does God exist? If I submit to order, do I thereby lose my freedom? Virtue is a nice ideal, but the path of least resistance is irresistible. And as for cooperation, why should I sacrifice opportunities for myself in the interest of others who have little or no regard for me? As former Supreme Court Justice Earl Warren once remarked, "I always turn to the sports pages first, which records people's accomplishments. The front page has nothing but man's failures". The successes in the world of sports can easily outshine the dismal record of daily life.

We can easily excuse our own moral failures, though we demand perfection from our sports heroes. This anomaly may be explained, at least in part, by the fact that we love to observe what may be too difficult for us to achieve. In other words, we love to witness something for which we are capable, but lack the motivation to accomplish. We project our better selves onto the TV screen and applaud what we could be. We identify more with our sports heroes than we do with ourselves. Hence the lucrative sales of sports jerseys with the names of our heroes emblazoned on them. In our own personal lives we tend to be sluggish. "Most people," according to William James, "never run far enough on their first wind to find out they've got a second".

St. Paul urges us to transfer the virtues of sport to the energies of life. In I Corinthians (9:24-27) he makes the following statement:

> Do you not know that in a race all the runners run, but only one gets the prize? Run in such a way as to get the prize. Everyone who competes in the games goes into strict training. They do it to get a crown that will not last, but we do it to get a crown that will last forever. Therefore I do not run like someone running aimlessly; I do not fight like a boxer beating the air. No, I strike a blow to my body and make it my slave so that after I have preached to others, I myself will not be disqualified for the prize.

Hall of Fame coach Vince Lombardi was fond of citing St. Paul to motivate his players. Lombardi, a daily communicant throughout his life (as was his father) and a Fourth Degree Knight of Columbus, understood that life is more important than the game. Vatican II echoed this notion of striving in stating that:

> All the faithful of Christ are invited to strive for the holiness and perfection of their own proper state. Indeed they have an obligation to strive.

Lombardi modified the reference to perfection when he famously remarked that "Perfection is not attainable. But if we chase perfection, we can catch excellence". He had a talent for aphorisms. "Winners never quit," he said, "and quitters never win". "The only place success comes before work is in the dictionary." Lombardi led his Green Bay Packers to three straight NFL championships and, in 1966 and 1967, the first two Super Bowl victories.

We love to watch team sports because we find therein an image of our better selves. The Catholic Church, however, enjoins us to be our better selves. Sports may provide an inspiration for us to be that better self. In that case, it realizes a more important victory than whatever trophies and pennants it can win.

HOPE

One of the stormiest, if not the stormiest cape in the world is the Cape of Good Hope located off the southern tip of Africa where the powerful currents of the Atlantic and Indian oceans converge. When Portuguese navigator Bartolomeu Dias discovered this Cape in 1488, he called it, fittingly, the Cape of Storms. Later, King John II of Portugal renamed it "Cape of Good Hope" in anticipation of finding a sea route to India. Vasco da Gama proved his king to be prophetic when he sailed around the Cape of Good Hope and discovered the long sought after passage to India.

In this chronicle, history and symbolism come together. The hope of finding a sea route to India was eventually fulfilled only because hope had been kept alive. This is the historical fact. But added to this fact is the symbolism of hope being a "good hope" because it is born in an atmosphere of difficulty.

The stormy cape provided the crucible in which hope was tested and purified so that it could emerge precisely as "good hope". "Hope never spread her golden wings," wrote Ralph Waldo Emerson, "but in unfathomable seas".

We need "good hope" in our present era when the pandemic and the darkening sky are sources of discouragement and despair. Such a hope requires the qualities of realism, courage, patience, and the willingness to endure difficulties.

"Good hope" is contrasted with the many superficial hopes that get us through the day. We hope for good weather, that our home team will win, that we will get a raise, or that we will win the lottery. These hopes are little more than wishes. Our hope should be directed toward better things. We hope to be faithful to our friends, to achieve both our earthly and heavenly destinies.

We should not be defeated by difficulty. When we lose hope we find ourselves, as Dante stated, already in Hell. "Abandon hope, ye who enter here" are the words he inscribed over the entranceway to Hell (*Lasciate ogni speranza, voi ch'entrate.*). As long as we live, we should never abandon hope.

WHAT HISTORY CAN TEACH US

We live in the moment. We may dream of the future. But we can learn from the past. It is a grave mistake to look at the world today in isolation from the past. Such a viewpoint can be disheartening. Secularism is omnipresent. It engulfs us; it is the very substance of our day to day activities. The Covid-19 pandemic adds to our dismay. We wonder if God has abandoned us. The moment can be suffocating.

But this moment in time, like any other moment, is transitory. It does not possess the qualities of stability and permanence. Our nature as human beings, however, remains the same. When we read Dante's *Divine Comedy*, we easily understand the moral categories of good and evil that he describes and how they apply to all men. The allusions he makes to the peculiarities of his own moment are the passages that are not so easy to grasp. Plato and Aristotle make perfect sense to us when they write about truth, goodness, and justice, though they wrote more than 2,000 years ago. Times change, but the human person endures.

If the problems of the day seem overwhelming, we should remember that the human soul that yearns for happier days, retains its underlying strength. Although it may be somewhat muted in today's world, it will, as history has clearly shown, ultimately be revitalized and assert itself. We may say the same thing about the Catholic tradition. It has not disappeared, but will reassert herself in due time. As the great historian Christopher Dawson has noted, "Human nature always retains its spiritual character—its bond with the transcendent and the divine". The concerted attempt by communists to annihilate this character in Europe has failed miserably. Materialism in the secular world will inevitably, in time, also meet with failure. God has not turned Himself away from our current predicament and left us to grovel in spiritual darkness. We cannot abandon hope in His providential care.

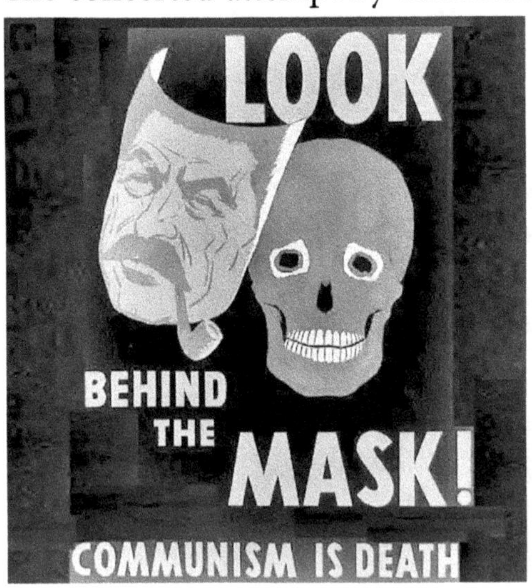

The distinguished historian Arnold Toynbee has stated that the tension between the claims of individual souls and the universal society is an inescapable issue. As a society moves toward a socialist or totalitarian state, the individual becomes increasingly unimportant.

This is not so much the case with the Catholic Church. The Church, despite its hierarchical structure and the fact that its millions of adherents stretch across the globe, remains ever open to the nourishment that an individual person can provide. We think of St. Bernadette and how this uneducated peasant girl played an important part not only in reinvigorating the religious life in France, but of the entire Catholic world. Her privileged relationship with Mary the Mother of God brought the notion

of the Immaculate Conception as an official dogma into the Church. We also think of the great contributions to Catholicism made by the children in Fatima or St. Ignatius Loyola, St. Francis Xavier, St. Teresa of Avila or St. John of the Cross. The Church does not lose sight over the infinite importance of the individual soul.

The Church produces saints because it is staunchly opposed to any kind of totalitarian regime. This, also, is a lesson from history. Who will be the saints of today that will once again, like St. Francis of Assisi, rebuild the Church? If we do not as yet know their names, we can trust that they will arrive (or have already arrived) and bring to the Church a new dawn. The folly of the present moment has neither the strength nor the imagination to sustain itself. The enduring realities will ultimately prevail.

What Should We Hope For?

While we are in the grip of the pandemic, we hope that it will soon be over so that we can return to a normal way of life. This hope is perfectly understandable. It is on the minds and hearts of virtually everyone. Yet, was that "old normalcy" not a precursor to the present pandemic, containing the very seeds that produced it? We need a more far-reaching and longer-lasting hope. If the pandemic was nothing more than an interruption between two periods of normalcy, it was entirely meaningless. We need a

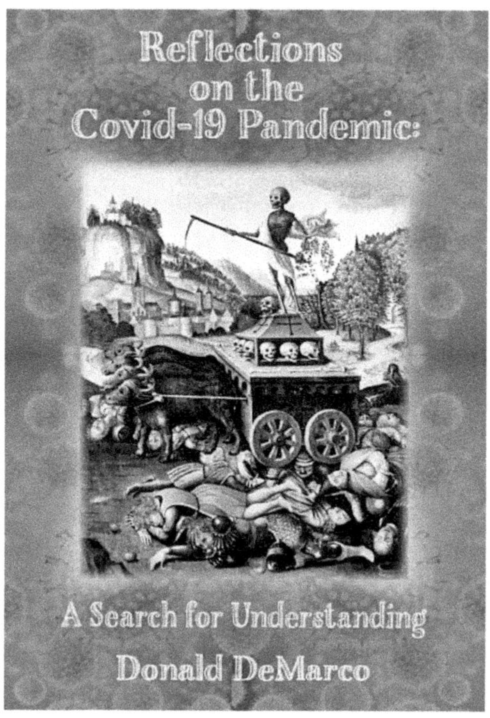

stronger, more demanding hope, one that finds a meaning to the pandemic, one that heralds a better, wiser, and more spiritually enriched life. We need to benefit from what the pandemic can teach us. We do not want it to prepare the way for another one of its kind. We cannot be satisfied with the pandemic coming to an end. Our hope is for more than its termination, but for the beginning of a richer and more humanly satisfying life.

The tragedy of the pandemic can be measured by the number of lives it has claimed, which is in the millions. This tragedy must be offset by a renewed appreciation and love of life. If we have not benefited from this present disaster, we will welcome, though unintentionally, another one. Our immediate hope for relief must be followed by a hope for a life that is far better than the "old normalcy".

Our hope is that the present pandemic serves as a catalyst that assists in a conversion of the heart. Our fear is that it will bring about discouragement that leads to an increase in suicide, abortion, and euthanasia. Our hope, therefore, must be stronger than our fear. History offers us inspirational characters who were able to advance through suffering from anonymity to greatness. We offer the examples of St. Paul of Tarsus, Fedor Dostoevsky, and John Keats.

Saul, whose name was later changed to Paul, was on his way to Damascus seeking to imprison whatever Christians he might encounter. Suddenly a brilliant flash of light from heaven struck him, knocking him to the ground. He heard the voice of Jesus speak to him: "Saul. Saul, why do you persecute me?" "Who are you, Lord?" Saul asked. "I am Jesus, whom you are persecuting," He replied. "Now get up and go into the city and you will be told what you must do" (Acts 9: 1-19). The men traveling with Saul were speechless. Since Saul was blinded by the light, his companions led him by the hand into Damascus. For three days, Saul could not see and did not eat or drink. God appointed Ananias to enter the house where Saul

was praying. "Brother Saul, the Lord — Jesus, who appeared to you on the road as you were coming here — has sent me so that you may see again and be filled with the Holy Spirit." Immediately, something like scales fell from Saul's eyes, and he could

see again. He got up and was baptized, and after taking some food, he regained his strength. After spending several days in Damascus, he began his life as perhaps the greatest preacher of the Word of the Lord who ever lived. His epistles make up 13 books of the New Testament. Paul's great mission was prepared for him by God through suffering and deprivation. The epistles of St. Paul constitute 25% of the New Testament. The 17th century mystical poet Thomas Traherne reminds us that "A Christian is an oak flourishing in winter."

In 1847, Fyodor Dostoevsky was an atheist who met with other like-minded individuals to discuss radical political ideas. He and his comrades were arrested, imprisoned for eight months and sentenced to death. The firing squad execution was a hoax, but it had its terrifying effect on Dostoevsky and his associates. One of them went mad. What eventuated for the young Russian writer was four years of exile in penal servitude in Siberia followed by an indefinite period as a common soldier. One book was allowed to the prisoners. Fortunately, for Dostoevsky, it was the Bible. Under harrowing conditions, the teachings of Christ and the spirituality of the Russian Orthodox Church took deeper meaning for Dostoevsky. He came to understand his misfortunes as an opportunity to gain salvation through suffering. His tenure in prison provided him with rich material that he would later use in his novels. "The only thing I fear is that I will not be worthy of my own suffering" became his enduring maxim.

John Keats experienced twin sufferings: alienation from his loved ones in England and tuberculosis. "This world," he

writes, "is not simply a 'vale of tears' but a vale of soul-making" There may be sparks of divinity in millions of people, but they are mere intelligences until they attain their true identity, until they are personally themselves. How, then, does one become a 'soul'? "Do you not see," he reasons, "How necessary a world of pains and troubles is to school an intelligence and make it a soul?" It was clear enough for the young poet that suffering has meaning. It is the necessary medium through which a mere individual gains his rightful self, his soul. Keats did not, as he once feared, write his name on 'water', but carved a name that posterity cannot forget.

St. Paul became Christianity's greatest apostle, Dostoevsky, Russia's greatest novelist, and John Keats, England's greatest lyric poet. Their transformations (or conversions) required the purification of their personalities through the crucible of suffering. The current pandemic, no doubt, is providing similar transformations for many. It need not be seen as all gloom, but as a real possibility for changing a complaining individual into a creative personality.

The Power of Words

The adage that the pen is mightier than the sword is testament to the power of words. The right words can change a person's life and place him on a better course. Scripture is replete with powerful verbal phrases that can inspire comfort, courage, and confidence. Consider the following five-word phrases culled from the Bible: "I will be with you" (Isaiah 43:2). "My peace I give you" (John 14: 27). "I will not forget you" (Isaiah 49:27). "I will give you rest" (Matthew 11:28). "You are precious and honored" (Isaiah 43:4).

Words can be an inspiration on an everyday level for ordinary people. But they can also be an important inspiration for those who are well known.

A young man was talking to a close friend and telling her that all he wanted was to find the right person. Without missing a beat, she said, "Everybody is looking for the right person, and nobody is trying to be the right person". The remark stopped the young man in his tracks. He suddenly realized that he should be the right person someone else is looking for. His perspective shifted from placing his expectations on others, which he could do nothing about, to himself. His life then took on a new direction, one of self-improvement.

Chris Norton was an 18-year-old college football player when a tackle he made left him paralyzed. After emergency surgery, doctors gave him a mere 3% chance if ever moving below his neck. On his fourth night in the hospital, a physician came to see him and did something that is not found in a medical textbook. She knelt down next to his bed and said, "Chris, look me in the eyes". "I'm here to tell you," she stated with irresistible conviction, "You will beat this. You will beat this". Her words restored his faith. From then on, he grew stronger, day by day. It was a slow improvement but he was finally able to walk. A few years later, he had enough strength to walk his bride down the aisle. He is now a motivational speaker, author, philanthropist, and father of seven. Four words changed his life forever.

St. Augustine's life was at a low ebb. He characterized himself as the most learned and most dissolute graduate of the University of Carthage. His life had been given over to lust. One day, while in his garden, he heard a child's voice say "*tolle lege*" (take and read). He had been reading the Letters of St. Paul and let the book open on its own. The book opened to the thirteenth chapter of the Letter to the Romans, where Paul exhorts his readers to give up the way of the senses and follow the path of Christ. These two words marked the turning point of his life. He became a Christian and embarked on a remarkable path in which he became a bishop, a Doctor of the Church and a saint.

Sergei Rachmaninoff's first symphony was met with scorn. Cesar Cui, one the formidable "Russian Five," commented that the 24-year-old composer must have studied in a "conservatory in hell". The negative reception left him unable to compose anything of substance for three years. He became an insomniac, lost his appetite, and spiraled into melancholia. At the advice of his aunt, he sought the help of Dr. Nikolai Dahl, a music-loving psychiatrist. Dahl placed Rachmaninoff under hypnosis and repeated to him day after day "You will begin to write your concerto . . . you will work with great facility . . . it will be excellent". The treatment was successful. "Although it may sound incredible," Rachmaninoff later recalled, "By autumn I had finished the first two movements of the Concerto". Rachmaninoff's Second Piano Concerto, which he dedicated to his esteemed doctor, is regarded as one of the truly great piano pieces, and takes its rightful place along with the concertos of Brahms, Beethoven, Mozart, and Chopin.

Patrick Peyton was a seminarian studying for the priesthood for the Congregation of the Holy Cross when he developed a severe case of tuberculosis. After spending several months flat on his back, his condition worsened. Doctors contemplated a desperate procedure which would save his life but leave him a permanent cripple. At this critical point Fr. Cornelius J. Hagerty came to visit him, "the man who," as Peyton would later state, "made the decisive contribution in what I regard as the supreme crisis and turning point of my life". His old philosophy professor was a man of absolute sincerity. Therefore, Peyton was well disposed to accept what he had to tell him. "Our Lady will be as good to you as you think she is," Fr. Hagerty said. "If you think she is a fifty-percenter that is what she will be; if you think she is a hundred-percenter, she will be for you a hundred-percenter." Peyton prayed to Our Lady with renewed confidence. In due time, after Hagerty's visit, doctors were astonished to find that the pernicious fluid was gone and confessed that they had no way of accounting for Peyton's dramatic improvement. The cure was total and the malady never recurred. He decided to spend the rest of his life devoted to the promotion of the rosary. The Family Rosary Crusade was born and Fr. Patrick Peyton brought the message that "the family that prays together stays together" to the four corners of the world. In 1961 he addressed a gathering of 550,000 people in San Francisco. That same year he spoke to 600,000 in Caracas, Venezuela. Fr. Peyton continued his crusade for more than 50 years. He was resurrected through words and wanted to provide the world with words of hope and trust.

We should never underestimate the power of words.

Getting Beyond Transgenderism

The current obsession with transgenderism in America has created a great deal of confusion. Are there no longer two distinct sexes? Is Genesis no longer a reliable authority? Or is it the case that sex is fluid and the sexes are interchangeable? Is one's sex simply a matter of choice? Is sex change a "right," even for minors?

In addition to disseminating a confusing message, transgenderism intimidates any dissenters. People have lost their jobs for insisting that there are but two sexes — male and female. Transgenderism is now the official doctrine. Those who argue against it do so at their own peril. President Biden's nominee for Secretary of Health is a man who has transgendered to a woman, "Rachel" Levine.

The recent *Equality Act* which permits biological males to compete in sports with biological females may be better understood as the Identity Act, asserting that the genders are fundamentally the same, an assertion that denies the once irrefutable argument that nature has made. It is now possible for a "man" to be a mother.

Ryan Anderson's book, *When Sally Became Harry*, purports to show that the push toward transgenderism is basically ideological and not based on sound medical science. Anderson is the president of the Ethics and Public Policy Center think-tank in Washington, D. C. Nonetheless, despite his qualifications, Amazon has banned his book. Ideology can be compelling when it is relentlessly promoted by the major media. Science must be compromised if it stands in the way of a blanket approval of transgenderism

Fortunately, Catholics do not need to fall into this confusing trap. They have clear models of motherhood and fatherhood, masculinity and femininity, in the persons of Mary the Mother of God and her spouse, St. Joseph. As models of the categorical difference between female and male, they serve as archetypes that bring needed light to a darkening world.

Mary and Joseph embody two qualities that are at the same time distinct and complementary. Mary is a "shelter" to her Son. Joseph is a "protector" who safeguards against danger. An angel told Joseph to "Rise up, take with thee the Child and His Mother and flee to Egypt". Joseph's role was to protect his family from Herod and he was obedient to the angel's command

(Matthew 2: 13).The words "shelter," as used here, and "protector," have different shades of meaning that sometimes overlap. "Shelter," in this instance, refers to providing comfort, whereas "protector" refers to providing safety. St. Joseph was protecting his family when he led them out of harm's way. These two terms are complementary. The message they offer to today's world of easy abortion is that the father should protect the life of his child, while the mother shelters it. The womb is a sanctuary, not an abortuary. Mary and Joseph speak to all mothers and to all fathers.

Edith Stein took the name Teresa Benedicta of the Cross when she entered the Carmelite order. She was canonized on October 11, 1998 by Pope John Paul II. She gave a great deal of thought to the problems between the sexes. These problems, she maintained, would persist until men and women adopted a supernatural remedy. She wrote:

> This transcendence of natural barriers is the highest effect of grace; it can never be achieved by carrying on a self-willed struggle against nature and denying its barriers, but only by humble subjection to the divine order.

Referring to the woman in particular, she stated that:

> The woman's soul is fashioned as a shelter in which other souls may unfold.

The eminent Swiss psychiatrist Carl Jung affirmed this sentiment when he wrote the following:

> This is the mother-love, which is one of the most moving and unforgettable memories of our lives, the mysterious root of all growth and change; the love that means homecoming, shelter, and the long silence from which everything begins and in which everything ends.

If there is another word that adds further clarification to the word "shelter," it is "tenderness". Nathaniel Hawthorne could not have expressed the matter more beautifully:

> I have always envied the Catholics their faith in that sweet, sacred Virgin Mother, who stands between them and the Deity, intercepting somewhat of His awful splendor, but permitting His love to stream upon the worshiper, more intelligibly to human comprehension, through the medium of a woman's tenderness.

Pope Francis would be in agreement with Hawthorne. In his *Ave Maria: The Mystery of a Most Beloved Prayer*, he states that:

> Wherever a mother is, there is tenderness. And Mary shows us with her motherhood that humility and tenderness are not virtues of the weak, but of the strong.

The notion of tenderness attributed to the Mother of God has been extremely popular throughout the centuries. The St. Vladimir icon, which dates back to the 12th century, is also known as *Our Lady of Tenderness*. It is generally considered to be one of the most cherished symbols in Russian history. In succeeding centuries, it has inspired many imitations. They all feature the loving tenderness that is expressed between Mary and her Son. Consistently, the Mother of God is looking at the viewer as if to invite all mothers to imitate the tenderness she has for her child.

Mary and Joseph are role models who personify a number of virtues that all women and men should adopt. The war between the sexes and all the confusion it generates is the inevitable consequence of denying the relevance of the supernatural. God created two sexes. But He also created Mary and Joseph to epitomize them. The fact that the president of the United States, who declares himself to be a Catholic, is far at sea on this matter, is a scandal of inestimable proportions.

Ten Things To Remember Before Deciding Not To Return To Mass

During the Covid-19 pandemic many Catholics have been deprived of attending Mass. This deprivation has been ongoing for months, enough time for some Catholics to begin to think that the Mass is no longer central to their lives. It is important to remember, however, what one is giving up in deciding, after a long quarantine, not to return to Mass. The following offers ten important reasons for returning to Mass that Catholics need to take seriously.

1) The four primary reasons for attending Mass:

The Mass offers us the opportunity to worship God in an appropriate environment and in a most appropriate way, to ask for His forgiveness, to thank Him for the many blessings He has bestowed upon us, and to ask for the grace to be ever faithful to Him. These four points can be summed up in the acronym ACTS, representing Adoration, Contrition, Thanksgiving, and Supplication.

2) The Eucharist as spiritual nourishment:

The reception of the Holy Eucharist is the reception of Christ and offers a more abundant life: "I am the living bread that came down from heaven. Whoever eats of this bread will live forever; and the bread that I will give for the life of the world is my flesh" (John 6:51). There is no better spiritual food for Catholics than what they receive in the Eucharist. The Church lives by the gift of the life of Christ.

3) Praying as a community:

Attending Mass gives us the opportunity to pray with others. Communal prayer, as opposed to solitary prayer, is more in line with the prayer of the Church as a whole and in conformity with the Communion of Saints. In joining prayer to song, as Augustine states, "he who sings prays twice".

4) Praying for the Church:

Prayer is the life-blood of the Church. As such it radiates outward to the whole world, asking for blessings that enable the Church to carry out its divinely appointed mission. Praying for the Church has a wider scope than is the objective of individual prayers. Catholics are privileged to be part of a universal activity that brings grace to people and situations of which they may be unaware.

5) Invoking the saints:

During the Mass, the saints of the church are invoked.

Saints offer testimony that a truly Christian life is attainable. We ask for their own prayers as we seek to imitate their example. St. Mary Mother of God, St. Francis of Assisi, St Teresa of Avila, St. Dominic, St. Thomas Aquinas, St. Ignatius, and many others offer us the assurance that being in their company is a great blessing.

6) Honoring the dead:

Those who have passed away are remembered. They should not be forgotten as members of the Mystical Body of Christ. They may be in need of our prayers. The Church includes both the living and the dead and is a continual reminder that the life of the deceased, as is our own, is everlasting. The Mass is a prayer for everyone and for all time.

7) Living the church calendar:

The Mass takes us through the liturgical year consisting of six seasons. Advent is the four-week period in preparation for Christmas. Lent is the six-week period prior to Easter and the Sacred Paschal Triduum. Ordinary Time includes the periods after Christmas and after Easter. The liturgical Calendar reminds us that we are involved in a spiritual cycle in which we relive the life of Christ. It adds spirituality to our ordinary secular year.

8) Receiving grace to amend one's life:

We approach Mass with a certain humility, mindful of our sins and indiscretions. It is a time to be honest with ourselves and ask God to help us in the coming days. The Mass, therefore, becomes a stepping stone to a better and more spiritual life. We should exit from Mass with a sense of a renewed spirit, better prepared to meet the challenges of the world.

9) Re-establishing a good habit:

After not attending Mass for a long period of time, we inherit the danger of being infected by the deadly sin of sloth.

This vice is not simply laziness, as is commonly believed, but the reluctance or the refusal to involve oneself in spiritual activities. Abstaining from Mass invites the bad habit of lapsing into a self-centered and non-spiritual mode of living. Regular attendance at Mass forms a good habit and a discipline that is most beneficial.

10) Being an example and a witness for others:

The temptation to avoid Mass on a regular basis is challenged by those who return to Mass who might prod the delinquents into returning. Good example can offset laziness in others. In addition, one may be a witness to the benefits derived from attending Mass. There should be a palpable and perhaps even contagious joy that the Mass-goer exemplifies.

1 Corinthians 1:18-25

The language of the cross may be illogical to those who are not on the way to salvation, but those of us who are on the way see it as God's power to save. As scripture says: I shall destroy the wisdom of the wise and bring to nothing all the learning of the learned. Where are the philosophers now? Where are the scribes? Where are any of our thinkers today? Do you see now how God has shown up the foolishness of human wisdom? If it was God's wisdom that human wisdom should not know God, it was because God wanted to save those who have faith through the foolishness of the message that we preach. And so, while the Jews demand miracles and the Greeks look for wisdom, here are we preaching a crucified Christ; to the Jews an obstacle that they cannot get over, to the pagans madness, but to those who have been called, whether they are Jews or Greeks, a Christ who is the power and the wisdom of God. For God's foolishness is wiser than human wisdom, and God's weakness is stronger than human strength.

From a letter by St Boniface

In her voyage across the ocean of this world, the Church is like a great ship being pounded by the waves of life's different stresses. Our duty is not to abandon ship but to keep her on her course.

Since the truth can be assaulted but never defeated or falsified, with our tired mind let us turn to the words of Solomon:

> Trust in the Lord with all your heart and do not rely on your own prudence. Think on him in all your ways, and he will guide your steps.

Let us stand fast in what is right and prepare our souls for trial. Let us wait upon God's strengthening aid and say to him: O Lord, you have been our refuge in all generations.

Let us be neither dogs that do not bark nor silent onlookers nor paid servants who run away before the wolf. Instead let us be careful shepherds watching over Christ's flock. Let us preach the whole of God's plan to the powerful and to the humble, to rich and to poor, to men of every rank and age, as far as God gives us the strength, in season and out of season.

Other Titles by Dr. DeMarco

Abortion in Perspective
Sex and the Illusion of Freedom
Today's Family in Crisis
The Anesthetic Society
The Shape of Love
The Incarnation in a Divided World
In My Mother's Womb
Hope for a World without Hope
Chambers of the Heart
How to Survive as a Catholic in a Parochial World
Character in a Time of Crisis
The Many Faces of Virtue
Timely Thoughts for Timeless Catholics
New Perspectives in Contraception
The Integral Person in a Fractured World
Patches of God-Light
The Heart of Virtue
Virtue's Alphabet from Amiability to Zeal
Biotechnology and the Assault on Parenthood
Architects of the Culture of Death
Being Virtuous in a non-Virtuous World
The Value of Life in a Culture of Death
A Family Portfolio in Poetry and Prose
How to Flourish in a Fallen World
In Praise of Life
How to Remain Sane in a World That Is Going Mad
Ten Major Moral Mistakes and How They Are Destroying Society
Poetry That Enters the Mind and Warms the Heart
Footprints in the Sands of Time
Why I Am Pro-Life and Not Politically Correct
Notes from the Underground: Dialogue with a World in Disarray
Apostles of the Culture of Life
How to Navigate Through Life
A Moral Compass in a World of Confusion
Reflections on the Covid-19 Pandemic
The War Against Civility
12 Supporting Pillars of the Culture of Life and Why They Are Crumbling

www.ingramcontent.com/pod-product-compliance
Ingram Content Group UK Ltd.
Pitfield, Milton Keynes, MK11 3LW, UK
UKHW021918190726
13853UKWH00002B/729